AF619167

The Ransomware War

The Ransomware War

Russian Cybergangs and the Defense of U.S. Critical Infrastructure

Duane A. Long

Copyright © 2024 by Duane A. Long

All rights reserved.

No part of this book may be reproduced, stored in a retrieval system, or transmitted in any form or by any means, electronic, mechanical, photocopying, recording, or otherwise, without prior written permission of the author, except for brief quotations in reviews or scholarly works permitted under U.S. copyright law.

The information presented in this book is for educational and informational purposes only. The author makes no representations or warranties regarding the completeness, accuracy, or reliability of the information contained herein.

Descriptions of cyber incidents and techniques in this book are presented for analytical and educational purposes only and should not be interpreted as operational guidance.

The views expressed in this work are those of the author and do not necessarily reflect the views of any government agency, organization, or employer.

All trademarks and registered trademarks appearing in this book are the property of their respective owners.

ISBN: 979-8-234-03457-1

Cataloging Data

Long, Duane A.
The Ransomware War: Russian Cybergangs and the Defense of U.S. Critical Infrastructure / Duane A. Long. — First edition.

Includes bibliographical references and index.

1. Ransomware (Computer security) — United States.
2. Cybercrime — Russia (Federation).
3. Computer networks — Security measures — United States.
4. Critical infrastructure — Security measures — United States.
5. National security — United States.

First Edition
First published in the United States in 2024

Printed in the United States of America

10 9 8 7 6 5 4 3 2 1

Dedication

For everyone who saw more in me than I saw in myself.

Don't be afraid to do something just because it's impossible.

—Kobi Yamada

Table of Contents

Preface

Over the past decade, ransomware has evolved from a relatively obscure form of cybercrime into one of the most significant cybersecurity threats facing governments, corporations, and critical infrastructure systems worldwide. What was once a nuisance affecting individual computer users has developed into a sophisticated criminal enterprise capable of disrupting essential services, threatening national economies, and undermining public trust in digital systems.

This book originated as doctoral research examining ransomware attacks conducted by cybercriminal organizations operating from within Russia against critical infrastructure in the United States. Portions of this work were originally published in 2024 under the title *Countering Russian Cybergang Ransomware Attacks Against Critical Infrastructure in the United States*. During the course of that research, it became increasingly clear that ransomware attacks represent more than isolated criminal incidents. Rather, they reflect a broader strategic challenge created by the intersection of cybercrime, geopolitical competition, and the increasing digitalization of modern infrastructure.

Modern societies depend on complex networks of interconnected digital systems that control energy production, transportation, communications, healthcare, and financial services. While these systems offer enormous efficiency gains, they also create new vulnerabilities. Cybercriminal organizations have proven remarkably adept at exploiting those vulnerabilities, often operating from jurisdictions where enforcement is limited or where authorities may tolerate such activities for strategic reasons.

The research presented in this book examines the evolution of ransomware as a form of cyber extortion. This ecosystem allows cybercriminal groups to operate at scale and poses a growing threat to critical infrastructure in the United States. Drawing on case studies and analyses of ransomware incidents affecting corporate, government, and military institutions, the work explores both the operational characteristics of ransomware attacks and the policy challenges they pose for national security.

In addition to analyzing the threat environment, this book evaluates potential strategies for improving the United States' ability to defend critical infrastructure against ransomware attacks. As cyber threats continue to evolve, effective responses will require coordination across government agencies, private industry, and international partners. Addressing the ransomware challenge is not simply a matter of improving cybersecurity practices; it also involves broader questions of policy, deterrence, and international cooperation.

While this work originated as academic research, its purpose is ultimately practical. The ransomware threat is not theoretical. It has already disrupted energy supplies, medical systems, transportation networks, and government operations. Understanding how these attacks occur—and how they might be prevented—is essential to protecting the digital infrastructure upon which modern society depends.

Dr. Duane A. Long

Introduction

On May 7, 2021, fuel deliveries across much of the eastern United States abruptly stopped. Gas stations from Georgia to Virginia began running dry as drivers lined up for hours in panic buying that quickly spread across several states.

The disruption was not caused by mechanical failure or a natural disaster. Instead, the Colonial Pipeline—one of the most important fuel arteries in the United States—had been crippled by a ransomware attack carried out by the Russian cybercriminal group DarkSide. Within hours, a criminal organization operating thousands of miles away had disrupted a major segment of the American energy supply.

The Colonial Pipeline incident illustrated a troubling reality: modern societies now depend on digital systems that can be attacked from anywhere in the world. Criminal organizations no longer need armies, missiles, or even physical proximity to inflict significant damage on national infrastructure. A small group of skilled cybercriminals armed with malicious software can now disrupt pipelines, hospitals, financial systems, and government services.

Ransomware has evolved from a nuisance targeting individual computer users into a multi-billion-dollar criminal enterprise that threatens national economies and critical infrastructure. Many of the most sophisticated ransomware groups operate from within the Russian Federation, where they benefit from weak enforcement, political protection, or state tolerance that allows their activities to continue largely unhindered.

This book examines the growing ransomware threat to American critical infrastructure and explores strategies the United States may adopt to counter these attacks. Drawing on research on corporate, government, and military institutions affected by ransomware incidents, the analysis explores how cybercriminal organizations operate, why existing defenses often fail, and what policy options offer more effective protection.

Ultimately, the question facing policymakers is not whether ransomware attacks will continue—they will. The real question is whether the United States will adapt quickly enough to defend the digital systems that underpin modern life.

List of Abbreviations

BGH	Big Game Hunting
CISA	Cybersecurity & Infrastructure Security Agency
CNI	Critical National Infrastructure
CSIS	Center for the Study of Intelligence
CSS	Central Security Service
CTED	Counter Terrorism Committee Executive Directorate
CTIIC	Cyber Threat Intelligence Integration Center
DDoS	Distributed Denial-of-Service
DHS	Department of Homeland Security
DISA	Defense Information System Agency
DOD	Department of Defense
DODIN	Department of Defense Information Networks
DOE	Department of Energy
DOJ	Department of Justice
EPA	Environmental Protection Agency
FAA	Federal Aviation Administration
FBI	Federal Bureau of Investigation
GCHQ	Government Communications Headquarters
ICS	Industrial Control System
ISIS	Islamic State of Iraq and the Levant / Islamic State of Iraq and Syria
MCNA	Managed Care of North America
MCPA	Military Cyber Professionals Association
NATO	North Atlantic Treaty Organization
NCF	National Cyber Force
NCSC	National Cyber Security Centre
NCIJTF	National Cyber Investigative Joint Task Force

NIPRNet	Non-classified Internet Protocol Router Networks
NIST	National Institute of Standards and Technology
NSA	National Security Agency
ODNI	Office of the Director of National Intelligence
ONCD	Office of the National Cyber Director
SCADA	Supervisory Control and Data Acquisition
SSF	Strategic Support Force
TREAS	Department of the Treasury
U.N.	United Nations
UNOCT	United Nations Office of Counter Terrorism
USAF	United States Air Force
USCYBERCOM	United States Cyber Command
USSCCST	U.S. Senate Committee on Commerce, Science, and Transportation
USSS	United States Secret Service
VPN	Virtual Private Network

1

Introduction to the Ransomware Threat

Ransomware is malicious software (often shortened to malware) that encrypts data and demands a ransom to decrypt it. Essential documents, system files, and user interfaces (such as login screens) are examples of targets for encryption. After successfully infecting a computer, malware typically displays a message instructing the victim to pay the perpetrator to obtain access to the decryption keys. Each new generation of ransomware devised is more difficult to counter than the preceding iteration.[1] Ransomware enables individual bad actors to harm online information systems worldwide. Criminals pursue illegal endeavors with low risk yet high reward.[2] Online crimes are often difficult to trace but very profitable, so they meet these preferences. International cybergangs use ransomware as a low-risk, high-reward extortion technique to target victims across international boundaries.[3] The lucrative success of these crimes has prompted the formation of cybergangs that organize the mass spread of ransomware across the internet.[4] Russia allows and actively encourages its cybercriminals to operate freely across international boundaries.[5] It is difficult to counter this emerging threat, as Russia denies the existence of cybergangs operating within its borders.[6]

Additionally, Russia's refusal to acknowledge the presence of cybergangs has created a safe harbor for them to launch ransomware attacks with impunity, protected by the Russian Federation. In 2021, a ransomware attack by the Russian cybergang DarkSide disrupted gasoline distribution over the entire U.S. East Coast.[7] The United States government identifies 16 support divisions as critical infrastructure sectors, which provide "essential services that underpin American society":[8]

Chemical
Commercial Facilities
Communications
Critical Manufacturing
Dams
Defense Industrial Base
Emergency Services
Energy
Financial Services
Food and Agriculture
Government Facilities
Healthcare and Public Health
Information Technology
Nuclear Reactors, Materials, and Waste
Transportation Systems
Water and Wastewater Systems

The energy sector comprises natural gas, electricity, and oil, which includes gasoline.[9] The United States' policy is "to strengthen the security and resilience of its critical infrastructure against both physical and cyber threats."[10] The United States government desires to create a means to interdict ransomware attacks by Russian cybercriminals on America's critical infrastructure.

Background

Cybergangs increasingly target American businesses for ransomware attacks.[11] In 2021, the U.S. Treasury predicted Russian hackers would be responsible for 75% of all ransomware attacks.[12] According to research presented at the 2022 CYBERWARCON security conference, the Russian government actively monitors and directs the criminal activities of Russian cybergangs.[13] In 2021, over 30 nations collaborated to form the International Counter Ransomware Initiative—an institution to "address the ransomware threat and to press Russia to act against criminal ransomware activities emanating from its territory."[14] Despite their efforts, the number and scale of ransomware attacks originating in Russia continue to increase.[15]

Problem Statement

Research by Aurangzeb et al.[16] shows that cybercriminals target the United States more often than other nations worldwide. Companies throughout the United States, particularly those with networked critical infrastructure systems, are experiencing ransomware cyberattacks at an increasing pace.[17] Recent experience indicates that industries in the United States are falling victim to ransomware attacks at an ever-increasing rate—including network-connected critical infrastructure systems.[18] Despite new initiatives by agencies such as the FBI and the Treasury Department to curb ransomware, attacks on American networks continue to rise.[192021] The ubiquity of these escalating ransomware attacks led the United States government to declare this malware a threat to national security.[22]

Purpose Statement

Non-state actors' increasingly sophisticated cyberattacks can potentially threaten whole countries.[23] However, the recent ransomware attack on Colonial Pipeline shows that some nations may reject or ignore the criminal behavior of hackers operating within their borders.[24] This research aimed to understand how to better fight against ransomware cyberattacks perpetrated by Russian cybergangs within the Russian Federation's protected boundaries. The research examined historical and current ransom crimes to understand the ransomware phenomenon better.

The researcher also examined how private-sector organizations, government agencies, and the United States military fared in their efforts to counter ransomware attacks. The author analyzed the data to answer the research questions. This researcher characterizes these results as deterrents that lead to the cessation or a drastic reduction in successful ransomware incursions by Russian cybergangs, without risking a military confrontation with Russia.

Research Questions

What strategies can the United States federal government adopt and implement to thwart ransomware attacks on critical infrastructures by cybercriminal gangs operating from within Russia?

What is the impact of centralizing America's cyberdefense to thwart the spread of ransomware?

What kind of impact would creating a Cyber Force with a dual mission analogous to the Coast Guard's dual missions have on America's goal of countering ransomware threats?

Scope

Assumptions

This research assumed that ransomware attacks on America's critical infrastructure would continue to constitute a significant threat. Additionally, the researcher assumed that the success of past ransomware attacks would spur Russian cybergangs to continue and intensify their assaults on critical infrastructure within the United States.

Limitations

Some companies conceal information about hacks from the public;[25,26] therefore, not all information is openly available. Due to the information blackout, this research considered only publicly accessible data. Moreover, national security considerations limit public information on this topic. The United States government classifies certain national security defense efforts, limiting public information on current ransomware countermeasures.

Delimitations

This research examined a representative sample of cyberattacks against U.S. institutions, as investigating all occurrences would have required an exorbitant amount of time and resources.

Rationale

Globally, Russian ransomware attacks are rising in frequency and intensity. The Center for the Study of Intelligence (CSIS) monitors "[cyberattacks] against government institutions, the military, and high-tech enterprises, as well as economic crimes with losses exceeding $1 million."[27] According to their statistics, 96 successful attacks occurred worldwide between January and September 2022.[28] This figure is much higher than the 67 attacks reported in 2012 and the 27 assaults recorded in 2017.[29] Each year, the number of successful attacks increases globally.

Significance

Cybercriminals in Russia have evolved ransomware to the point that they may impair large portions of the nation.[30] In addition, the Russian government manipulates cybergang activities to advance official objectives through deniable asymmetric attacks against its opponents.[31] The intelligence community, counterterrorism experts, and law enforcement personnel must tackle this new threat.

Definitions and Key Terms

Critical infrastructure: foundational entities and resources essential to the safety, security, and normal operations of a nation.[32]

Cyberdefense: steps to detect, discriminate, dissuade, and minimize risks, as well as restore computers and networks to a secure configuration, are all included in this kind of cyber activity geared at repelling specific threats that have breached or have the potential to compromise computerized networks.[33]

Cyberattack: malicious online attacks on computer networks and systems with a denial-of-service impact.[34]

Cybercriminal: an online criminal who uses various computer networks to commit crimes.[35]

Cybersecurity: anything done online to prevent hackers from infiltrating networks and destroying data.[36]

Cyberspace: the technological ecosystem of interconnected information systems, digital data, electronic networks, and infrastructure.[37]

Cyberterrorist: someone who engages in terrorist actions using electronic networks.[38]

Cyberwarfare: the use of computer networks and information technology to attack and impair the operational capabilities of a nation.[39]

Extortionware: a form of ransomware that exfiltrates data in addition to encryption.[40]

Ransomware: malicious software that limits access to a computer system or its data until the user pays a ransom.[41]

SCADA (supervisory control and data acquisition): a type of information system used in a variety of areas for data gathering, data analysis, and the remote control of networked computers to aid administrators with the implementation of changes.[42]

State-connived: governments that feign ignorance of the actions, or existence, of malicious non-state actors active inside their borders and committing aggressive acts against other nation-states.

State-directed: entails non-state actors who operate at the behest of, or as instructed by, a government and receive substantial support from the government to conduct their operations.[43]

State-sponsored: autonomous non-state actors that receive support from the state while maintaining their autonomy.[44]

Organization of the Remaining Chapters

Chapter 2: The Evolution of Ransomware

This section gives an overview of the literature examining the ransomware conundrum. It reviews research on defensive and offensive measures to thwart ransomware attacks and how criminals have adapted their methods to circumvent them. The researcher analyzed the data to identify knowledge gaps regarding effective countermeasures at this stage.

Chapter 3: Research Methodology

This section discusses the approach the author used to perform the analysis. This research applied a grounded theory qualitative methodology, and a substantial portion involved studying and evaluating existing reports and data. This section examines the techniques used throughout this qualitative investigation. The section details case studies, data collection techniques, recent changes, analyst projections, the database the researcher created for the analysis, the types of sources the author utilized, and the data collection techniques.

Chapter 4: Analysis of Ransomware Attacks

In this chapter, the author describes the raw data results from the research. As this research examined ransomware instances across three industries—corporate entities, government agencies, and military branches—the author details how these institutions fared against ransomware attacks during the research period. The researcher details the results for each institution in a separate section of this chapter.

Chapter 5: Policy Implications

This final chapter encompasses an expository discussion on the meanings of research results. The researcher elaborates on the implications of the results and the conclusions drawn from them. The author concludes the chapter with recommendations for security practitioners, policymakers, and future researchers, based on the research results.

Ransomware Threat Introduction Summary

Everyday life in America depends on various forms of information systems. Some of these systems govern and control automated critical infrastructure operations (power grids, fuel services, and water purification serve as examples). These networked systems now face a constant siege by Russian cybergangs deploying ransomware attacks. The danger posed by ransomware to the United States grows daily, as does the potential damage it might do. Russia's unwillingness to address this problem worsens the issue. Consequently, the nation requires new initiatives to protect America's cybersecurity infrastructure. The United States must determine how to counter ransomware assaults by Russian cybergangs on America's critical infrastructure.

2
The Evolution of Ransomware

The increasing sophistication and reach of ransomware variants create a hegemony for Russian cybergangs. Russia colludes with cybergangs on the global ransomware crimes spawning from within its borders. As this research posits, this phenomenon may require national-level countermeasures against ransomware attacks launched from within the Russian Federation by cybergangs. It investigated responses to ransom events. This research aimed to ascertain if a means exists for Russian cybergang ransomware prevention, deterrence, reduction, or mitigation that does not risk a military confrontation with Russia.

In this chapter, the author examined previous research on interrelated ransomware issues to provide a current understanding of the problem. This examination encompassed:

- a historical assessment of the ransom phenomenon,
- reasons for attacks (when known),
- the emergence and proliferation of ransomware,
- the mechanics of ransomware,
- an analysis of the factors facilitating the effectiveness of ransom events,
- an overview of Russian ransomware,
- the standing cyber forces of various nations,
- and an assessment of ransomware interdiction theories.

The objective of this review was to identify gaps in the existing knowledge base on effective countermeasures against Russian cybergang ransomware.

Literature Review Methodology

Examining the existing knowledge base on ransomware required an in-depth exploration of scholarly databases for information pertinent to the phenomenon. The following describes the literature review methodology by outlining the primary search terms used and the principal databases searched.

Search Terms

The author used various search terms to collect and aggregate the information for this literature review. Applying Boolean operators, the researcher included searches for the phrases:

- *critical infrastructure + ransomware + cyber force*
- *critical infrastructure + ransomware*
- *Russia + critical infrastructure + ransomware*
- *Russia + cyberattacks + ransomware*
- *Russia + cyberattacks + cyber force*
- *cybercrime + ransomware*
- *cybercrime + critical infrastructure*
- *cyber force + cyberattacks + ransom*
- *cyber force + cyberattacks*
- *ransomware + origins*
- *ransom + history*
- *first uses of ransom*

Using these terms facilitated the accumulation of an extensive database of previous, interrelated research.

Databases Searched

The researcher examined academic journals, news media outlets, college databases, published books, government studies, and corporate reports for this review. The researcher vetted each source for quality and academic integrity to ensure it was appropriate for this research. However, the author excluded information from non-English sources due to potential translation issues.

Historical Use of Ransom

Merriam-Webster defines ransom as "to free from captivity or punishment by paying a price." [45] Conversely, the Cambridge Dictionary defines ransom as "a sum of money demanded in exchange for someone or something that has been taken." [46] Furthermore, Merriam-Webster defines ransomware as "a type of malware from cryptovirology that threatens to publish the victim's personal data or permanently block access to it unless a ransom is paid off."[47] Although ransomware is a relatively novel phenomenon, the tactic of demanding currency or valuables in exchange for the return of an object or person stretches back millennia. A brief historical review of ransom was germane to this research project, as it provided insight into ransomware.

Ransoming in the Ancient World

One of the more prominent examples of ransom in early history occurred in 75 BCE, when Cilician pirates abducted the 25-year-old Julius Caesar.[48] This event stood out for several reasons: it was an early, well-documented ransom case, the abduction of an important political figure, and Caesar's actions during the affair were atypical for a ransom situation. Although he was never an emperor, Caesar was one of the most notable leaders of ancient Rome. However, at the time of his capture, he had not ascended to the position of Rome's leader.[49]

The pirates demanded a ransom of 20 Roman talents for Caesar's safe return;[50] however, upon hearing this amount, Caesar reportedly balked and demanded they increase it to 50 talents (over $13 million).[5152] In his research, Lennox-Gentle noted that at this time, pirates kidnapping wealthy people, such as Caesar, for ransom, was a relatively common occurrence.[53] The pirates received their ransom, and Caesar returned safely home. Afterward, Caesar assembled a fighting force that tracked the pirates down and subsequently captured them for crucifixion.[54]

Ransoming through the 17th to 19th Centuries

The ransoming of valuable people and property continued over the centuries, and it increasingly became a profitable venture for criminals. This phenomenon reached incredible levels between 1575 and 1692, as Barbary pirates took thousands of hostages and demanded ransoms for their return.[55] Ambrus et al. studied this occurrence to glean insight into how European governments should contend with modern-day Somali pirates and ascertained a pronounced adverse correlation between governments' refusal to make concessions and the amounts abductors demanded as ransoms.[56]

By the late 1700s, American trade and shipping in the Mediterranean faced severe disruptions from Barbary pirates who captured ships, demanded ransoms for their return, and prompted the U.S. Congress to allot $80,000 to negotiate with the Barbary States.[57] Capturing two U.S. vessels and 21 crew members in 1785, the Barbary demanded a ransom of $60,000; however, the United States countered with an offer of only $4,200—resulting in a negotiating stalemate that lasted for a decade.[58] America continued to encounter problems with the Barbary Algiers until 1796, when the United States agreed to remit $642,500 and an annual stipend of supplies.[59] The Constitutional Rights Foundation noted that this contention with pirates seizing vessels and crews for ransom continued for years, with one of the highest ransoms coming in 1803 when Tripoli pirates demanded $3 million for the return of 300 U.S. Navy officers.[60]

Records indicate that ransoming was not confined to the high seas. A 2013 article in Smithsonian Magazine detailed the discovery of the earliest known ransom note in American history.[61] The note, dated 1874, demanded $20,000 to return a kidnapped child.[62] The note warned, "if you put the cops hunting for him you is only defeeting yu own end [sic]."[63] However, Christian Ross did inform the police, who advised him against paying the ransom, believing it would only encourage other criminals to follow suit.[64] Christian Ross never paid the ransom, and the child, 4-year-old Charles Brewster Ross, never returned home.[65] No one was ever prosecuted for the kidnapping.[66]

These early crimes indicate that ransom was a common practice and that paying it led to the return of the people or property taken. At the same time, refusal or delays in ransom payments hindered or prevented the return of seized items. It was rare for authorities to locate and recover items taken for ransom successfully; however, they occasionally captured the criminals afterward and sometimes recovered the ransom.

Ransoming in the 20th Century

Detotto et al.[67] undertook a study to understand ransom kidnappings. Their study indicated that policies designed to deter ransom kidnappings yield mixed results.[68] They noted that, in principle, prohibiting a family from paying a ransom should result in fewer ransom kidnappings, and a lower expectation of attaining a ransom would lead to fewer abductions.[69]

The United States currently has a no-concessions policy in international kidnapping cases, and Jenkins[70] researched its effectiveness. The analysis found no evidence that a no-concessions policy affects the number of ransom kidnapping events.[71]However, Jenkins also noted that although the no-concessions policy may have failed to lower ransom kidnappings, it might have prevented more criminals from pursuing the criminal tactic.[72]

Pirates and criminals were not the only ones engaging in kidnapping for ransom, as it is a tactic that terrorists also practice. Shortland and Keatinge[73] endeavored to assess how various nations respond to terrorist ransom kidnappings. The research aimed to reduce the gap between U.N. policies on terrorist ransom payments and the actual practices of U.N. member nations. Shortland and Keatinge remarked that for terrorists, ransom kidnappings are a highly lucrative venture, as three individual terrorists were able to amass more than $155 million from multiple ransom kidnappings.[74] This research concluded that when the U.N. bans the practice of paying ransoms, yet individual member states continue to do so, it erodes the integrity and authority of the U.N. as a whole.[75]

The primary concern about paying ransom demands is that doing so merely encourages additional ransomware attacks. This view is a philosophy expressed by former U.S. Treasury Department Under Secretary for Terrorism and Financial Intelligence, David S. Cohen, "ransom payments lead to future kidnappings, and future kidnappings lead to additional ransom payments."[76] This stance echoed that of President Ronald Reagan when he stated, "America will never make concessions to terrorists—to do so would only invite more terrorism—nor will we ask nor pressure any other government to do so."[77] As such, modern terrorists shifted their practices from demanding ransoms to requesting prisoner exchange, which they believed Americans would find more palatable.[78]

Some Americans find it confusing that the United States will swap prisoners yet not pay ransoms to kidnappers.[79] However, the two situations differ in that the United States may elect not to pay a ransom, and the government does not prevent private individuals or groups (such as families) from paying a ransom if they choose to do so.[80] The Rand Corporation analyzed ransom events and found few connections between paying ransoms and the emergence of additional ransom events.[81]

Dutton[82] explored the complexities of paying ransoms to terrorist groups. Her research showed that despite the U.N. prohibition against paying terrorist ransom fees, terrorist groups still managed to collect over $100 million in ransom and were utilizing this money to fund continued campaigns against the nations they took money from.[83] Even when the G8 nations collectively agreed to stop paying ransom to terrorists, they knew it was an idea that was simpler on paper than in practice.[84] Meyer observed that in the five years between 2008 and 2013, Islamic extremist groups kidnapped more than 150 foreign nationals.[85] Meyer noted that a portion of the difficulty in getting the various nations to stop paying terrorists is that there is no agreed-upon definition for what constitutes a terrorist group.[86] As such, a group designated as a terrorist organization by one nation may be seen as a militant group by another. In addition, while nations may enter a situation with no desire to pay ransoms to terrorists, that situation may rapidly change when external political pressure emerges from the families, businesses, news media, and political rivals demanding that the government take action to ensure the return of their loved ones.[87]

At times, governments will attempt to make clandestine ransom payments to terrorists for the return of prisoners. This secrecy allows the government to maintain an official stance of not paying ransoms while facilitating citizens' safe return. The New York Times conducted an investigation that revealed that substantial sums of money were transferred from European countries to al Qaeda as a result of ransom payments for kidnappings.[88] The phenomenon had become so commonplace that kidnappings developed into one of al Qaeda's primary sources of revenue.[89] In an assessment of which European nations had likely secretly paid the ransom for the return of kidnap victims, France, Spain, Italy, Germany, Belgium, Denmark, Switzerland, and Sweden topped the list.[90]

Ransoming in the Digital Era

In the digital age, a new form of ransom emerged—ransomware. The earliest known form of ransomware was the 1989 AIDS Trojan, a computer virus.[91] Rather than spreading via networked information systems, the creator hid the AIDS Trojan virus on an infected floppy disk.[92] Once the Trojan infected a computer, it encrypted information and instructed the user to send $189 to a Panama post office box to receive the decryption keys.[93]

Emergence & Proliferation of Ransomware

As computers became increasingly commonplace, malicious actors continued to create and spread computer malware. Today's interconnected networks make it easier for criminals to deploy ransomware, preventing users from accessing critical systems and the information they contain. As such, it is appropriate to analyze how ransomware emerged and proliferated, as well as the rationale behind ransomware attacks.

Ransomware Emergence

Modern ransomware emerged in 2013 with the advent of CryptoLocker.[94] A selection of differing variants soon followed the success of this ransomware. Cybercriminals are constantly seeking new paths to spread their programs, and they have even targeted public libraries' information systems. [95] Phishing emails and malware attachments were the most common vectors for ransomware infections.[96] Complicating the issue is that we have moved beyond personal desktop computers. Contemporary cell phones are miniature computers; most modern televisions contain computers; and many homes have a litany of smart devices connected to the internet. Studying the evolution of ransomware, Mat et al. assessed that cybercriminals are now creating ransomware targeting cellular telephones running on operating systems such as Android.[97] Cellular phones often lack the same level of security as personal computers running Windows, Linux, or macOS, and their popularity makes them attractive targets for ransomware.[98]

Ransomware Proliferation

The success of the Stuxnet computer worm brought public attention to information systems such as supervisory control and data acquisition (SCADA) systems and industrial control systems (ICS).[99] These systems exist throughout the infrastructure that supports daily life in America (maintaining control over a host of critical sectors), yet they go largely unnoticed unless there is a problem. These systems are now among the primary targets of cybercriminals conducting ransomware attacks. Buchanan [100] reviewed recent cyberattacks on SCADA/ICS systems and determined that the primary method of protecting these systems is to adopt zero-trust policies to help eliminate vulnerabilities created by trusted users in error.

Richardson et al.[101] noticed that ransomware targeting has begun to shift. Early ransomware attacks primarily targeted individual consumers; however, that is no longer true. According to research by Richardson et al., cybercriminals now target organizations and institutions far more than individuals.[102] Furthermore, they noted that a significant share of ransomware targets government organizations.[103]

Ransomware Rationale

Researching the ransomware phenomenon, one ponders the rationale behind the attacks. Swasey[104] established that inadequate security invites ransomware attacks from those seeking to profit from them. She noted that increased cybersecurity training, preventive preparations, and larger budgets could decrease ransomware attacks in the healthcare industry.[105] While a lack of security may make an institution a tempting target, it does not answer why cybercriminals choose this method of attack.

Williams[106] addressed this matter directly by analyzing the motives of the Conti cybergang. This research indicated that cybercriminals opt for ransomware as a cost-effective, low-risk, high-reward crime that can be executed on a large scale.[107] However, this may not be their only rationale for the attacks. Holt et al.[108] focused their inquiry on the social networks of the cybercriminals who carried out the attacks. They were able to compile demographic data on typical ages and income levels, as well as on the locations where ransomware attacks predominantly originate—Russia. This project revealed that members of the community openly share information about their activities with one another, and, in the process, spur one another to greater misdeeds online.[109]

Investigating the links between Russian cybergangs and the Russian government, Nershi and Grossman concluded that there might be political rationales for cyberattacks, as the Russian government occasionally enlisted the aid of its domestic cybercriminals in state-connived network operations to influence events and engage in cyberwarfare against other nations.[110] With this in mind, it may seem natural that the Russian government would also recruit these same hackers to assist with the war in Ukraine. However, Weber[111] indicated that a lack of financial incentives deters Russian hackers from conducting large-scale ransom attacks on Ukraine.

The Mechanics of Ransomware

Understanding the specific characteristics and properties of ransomware is essential to this research. Accomplishing this requires understanding how ransomware is evolving, its functionality, how it spreads, its monetization, its links to organized crime, recent ransomware advancements, and its impacts. This review will foster a thorough understanding of the ransomware threat.

Evolution of Ransomware

Richardson and North[112] evaluated the evolution of ransomware, as well as mitigation and prevention techniques. They charted the progression of ransomware from the 1989 AIDS Trojan to the 2016 Locky attack.[113] This research is notable for revealing a pattern of ransomware development. Although ransomware initially affected only Windows operating systems, additional variants emerged that targeted Android and Apple devices.[114] While earlier versions used weak encryption that skilled users could circumvent, modern variants no longer have this vulnerability.[115]

Additionally, different ransomware variants would perform different encryption operations. Some ransomware versions would lock the computer screen, while others would encrypt various files on the hard drives, and others still would encrypt the hard drive itself.[116] The findings of Richardson and North parallel the conclusions of Muslim et al.[117]

In a 2021 study, Fernando et al. conducted similar research into the evolution, mitigation, and prevention of ransomware. The analysis delineated ransomware into two primary forms—cryptoransomware (which encrypts data on a computer) and locker ransomware (which locks a user out of the computer interface); however, both circulate in similar ways.[118] Fernando et al. discussed significant milestones in ransomware's evolution, including the shift to 2048-bit encryption in 2013.[119] The project concluded that modern technological innovations are driving the rapid evolution of ransomware.[120]

Conversely, during their investigation on ransomware evolution, Wadkar et al. discovered that hackers create most ransomware variants by rewriting the code of existing ransomware, adjusting the malicious code to circumvent the latest changes in information system security.[121] Alenezi et al. asserted that ransomware has evolved through five distinct stages, each with distinct characteristics and propagation methods.[122] The salient point here is not the unique characteristics or propagation methods, but rather that each successive stage resulted from new technological innovations that necessitated further advancement.[123]

Additionally, cybercriminals view devices running Android as ideal targets and create ransomware for them at ever-increasing rates.[1124] This is because tablets and cell phones utilizing Android software dominate the mobile device market.[125] However, as hackers create and adapt ransomware to exploit new technologies, it may be possible to anticipate future ransomware changes by predicting the adoption of emerging technologies. This change is the proposal by Tupadha and Stamp. [126] After researching the evolution of ransomware, they conceived a method in which programmers use machine learning to anticipate ransomware advancements.[127]

The final link in understanding ransomware evolution is to review how attack patterns have changed over the decades. This trend is a phenomenon that Zimba and Chishimba researched in 2019. This research concluded that the sophistication of ransomware attacks has continued unabated, and trends indicate that they will become increasingly challenging to prevent over time.[128]

How Ransomware Functions

Understanding how ransomware evolved from a minor annoyance to a critical threat is only one element of the problem; we must also comprehend how it functions. In the broad sense, most people might deduce that ransomware encrypts elements of an information system and prevents users from operating the computer as usual. However, this is a very generalized overview of ransomware functionality. Using ransomware, a cybercriminal typically "threatens to publish the victim's personal data or permanently block access to it unless a ransom is paid off."[129]

The malware presents a visual notification, informing victims that ransomware has locked their devices or encrypted their files.[130] In certain cases, ransomware attempts to propagate across networked systems.[131] Ransomware that does not employ encryption techniques impedes file access and system functionality.[132] Ransomware that uses encryption limits access to specific, high-value data. Extortionware is ransomware designed to encrypt and exfiltrate sensitive information, with cybercriminals threatening to release the data to the public if victims do not pay a designated sum.[133] Cellphone ransomware spreads through drive-by downloads or counterfeit applications, targeting mobile devices.[134] Cybercriminals pose a threat by potentially disclosing or selling exfiltrated information on the dark web.[135] There is a growing trend among cyber actors to demand payment in virtual currency in exchange for ransom.[136] The Secret Service information concurs with the data from a 2019 study by Anghel and Racautanu. Through their research, they concluded that there are four types of ransomware attacks, each functioning in a slightly different manner: encrypting ransomware, non-encrypting ransomware, leakware, and mobile ransomware.[137]

How Ransomware Spreads

Hull et al. examined the methods cybercriminals usually choose to deploy ransomware. By analyzing 18 different ransomware variants, they determined that email attachments are the most common vector for spreading ransomware; however, they also noted an emerging trend in which malicious links are replacing malicious attachments as the vector of choice.[138] This shift occurs because improved email filtering technologies prevent users from receiving malicious attachments.[139] However, despite improved filtering technologies, most ransomware attachments bypass filters designed to intercept them.[140]

How Cybercriminals Monetize Ransomware

Like all ransom events, ransomware requires transferring funds from a victim to a perpetrator. However, since ransomware events occur entirely in a virtual environment, the cybercriminal has little need to receive physical currency from the victim. Instead, most cybercriminals have turned to cryptocurrencies such as Bitcoin.[141] According to the findings of Custers et al.,[142] cybercriminals employ cryptocurrencies to conduct anonymous financial transactions, thereby evading detection by law enforcement authorities. After analyzing the economics of ransomware, Hernandez-Castro et al.[143] concluded that Bitcoin has greatly facilitated the success of modern ransomware operations.

Ransomware and Organized Crime

The lucrative nature of ransomware has inspired organized criminal gangs to adopt ransomware tactics as a new criminal endeavor. A study performed by O'Gorman and McDonald for the Symantec Corporation found that cybergangs are not collaborating on their ransomware activities.[144] However, instead, they are developing their ransomware independently of each other.[145] Additionally, these gangs recruit programmers to code newer, more potent ransomware.[146]

Impacts of Ransomware

Ransomware poses a severe threat to critical infrastructure in the United States.[147] The Colonial Pipeline attack illustrated how much havoc can arise from a single attack on a compromised information system.[148] Complicating matters even further, the ransomware variant that affected the pipeline was infectious. If Colonial had not shut down the systems, the infection could have spread to adjacent, networked systems.[149] Even when ransomware targets systems not critical to the nation's daily operations, it can still severely impede operations across an entire city. A recent ransomware attack successfully disrupted water, police, and court services in Dallas, Texas.[150]

Factors Facilitating the Effectiveness of Ransom Events

The United States faces an ever-increasing number of ransomware attacks. It is evident that ransomware threatens nations; however, one must ask why it is such a practical crime. The section analyzes the success of ransom crimes, how cybercriminals evade capture, the profitability of ransomware, and the vulnerabilities of American networks.

How Successful Are Ransom Crimes

One of the primary factors contributing to ransomware's success is the presence of company leaders who do not consider it a serious threat and take little to protect the organization from attacks. According to Scroxton's research, fewer than ¼ of company directors view ransomware as a concern for them or their companies.[151] This complacent attitude toward cybersecurity spreads from company heads to lower-level employees who do not take proper precautions when using computers.

Another factor facilitating ransomware success is that cybercriminals are becoming more savvy, choosing targets to do the most damage with their malicious code, such as energy production companies.[152] Not only are information systems in such locations updated far less frequently, but compromising them can also send a company into a crisis and force rapid capitulation to ransom demands.[153]

How Do Criminals Evade Detection and Capture?

In 2019, Afianian et al. researched the techniques cybercriminals utilize to avoid detection. The conclusions of this research showed that cybercriminals adopted evasive tactics to prevent their malware from falling into computer sandboxes, where the malicious code would be unable to affect an information system.[154] Another factor in favor of cybercriminals is the inherent anonymity of cryptocurrencies like Bitcoin—the currency of choice for ransomware attacks.[155] Aware of the difficulties in tracking and tracing Bitcoin payments, cybercriminals use cryptocurrencies to help obscure their identities. One of the most concerning factors helping cybercriminals avoid capture is that many cybergangs operate within nations, providing a haven or cover to conceal criminals' presence, as in Russia.[156]

Ransomware Profitability

Ransomware cybergangs operate primarily within Russia but exist in nations worldwide.[157] Individual cybergangs net millions of dollars annually from illicit ransomware activities.[158] Collectively, their ransoms bring in over half a billion dollars annually.[159] However, when discussing profiting from ransomware attacks, one sector that has gone nearly unnoticed is the cyber insurance industry. In the United States, the cyber insurance industry has become a sector with annual revenue exceeding $8 billion.[160]

American Computer Network Vulnerabilities to Ransomware

Projections indicate that ransomware attacks in the United States will continue to increase in frequency and severity.[161] Although the U.S. government has taken steps to shore up critical infrastructure vulnerabilities, American infrastructure remains highly vulnerable to ransomware attacks.[162] Additionally, even institutions entrusted with the safety and security of American citizens, such as police departments, are highly vulnerable to ransomware attacks, and cybercriminals are actively targeting them.[163] The research by Ryan et al. indicates that there will always be zero-day vulnerabilities and a delay in patching.[164] As a result, America's networks will always have vulnerabilities that cybercriminals can exploit.[165]

Russian Ransomware

This research centers on ransomware from Russian cybergangs, so examining the links between Russia and ransomware is appropriate. This section will assess the levels of ransomware spawning within Russia, review how cybergangs are involved with the ransomware problem, and investigate potential links between ransomware and the Russian government. Together, these components will provide a foundation for understanding Russian ransomware.

Ransomware Activity in Russia

The United States incurs numerous ransomware attacks from around the world, both foreign and domestic; however, most attacks in America are from Russia.[166] Abely[167] advocates a national policy of not negotiating with Russian cybercriminals to deter continued ransomware attacks.

Russian Cybergang Involvement

The United States government determined that the Russian cybergang DarkSide was responsible for the ransomware attack that crippled the Colonial Pipeline.[168][169] However, the recent high-profile ransomware assaults have made it difficult for these cybergangs to maintain a low profile.[170] With the cybercriminals drawing unwanted attention to themselves, the U.S. government has begun to make inroads in its war against Russian cybergangs.[171] Darkside, Conti, and Trickbot are some ransomware cybergangs that the U.S. government has identified and begun to combat.[172] To this end, the United States is now sanctioning individual members of these ransomware groups, leveling sanctions on seven members in February 2023.[173] These cybergangs are shifting tactics by subdividing themselves into smaller cells, making it more difficult for governments to fight them.[174]

Russian Government Involvement

Research results presented at the 2022 Cyberwarcon indicate that the Russian government oversees its cybercriminals' ransomware activities; however, the U.S. government has not formally corroborated this information.[175] Analyses indicate that the Russian government holds sway over these criminal groups, but the gangs remain and operate independently.[176]

National Cyber Forces

Nation-states typically address novel national security issues by assessing asset criticality, threats, and vulnerabilities to calculate risks, then making a risk tolerance decision and determining actions to mitigate or eliminate the threats. Subsequently, based on its assessments, decisions, and capabilities, each nation will take different steps to secure its interests in cyberspace. Ransomware is a form of malware, and malware is just one of the many threats countries must combat in cyberspace. At this stage, it is appropriate to examine the steps various countries have taken to defend their assets in the cyber domain—including those that have elected to create a standing cyber force.

Nations with Cyber Forces

As of this writing, the United Nations (U.N.) recognizes 193 nations worldwide.[177] However, only three countries possess a military branch designated as a cyber force—China, Germany, and Singapore.[178] Costello and McReynolds[179] examined the mission, capabilities, and structure of China's Strategic Support Force (SSF). Their research found that the SSF integrates the "space, cyber, electronic, and psychological warfare capabilities from across the [People's Liberation Army] services and its former General Departments" into a single cohesive whole.[180] As such, it cannot be defined as a dedicated cyber force. Analyzing the Cyber and Information Domain Service (Cyber- und Informationsraum) of Germany's Bundeswehr, Leinhos noted it as a proper, dedicated cyber organization created from the various cyber components of Germany's military and government sectors.[181] However, this organization operates strictly on military matters, and the defense of civilian cyber networks is the province of the Federal Office for Information Security.[182] In contrast, the research by Aigner et al. shows that the government of Singapore established the Digital and Intelligence Service to counter non-state actor threats originating in Russia.[183] In their exploration of Singapore's defense strategy, Matthews and Timur ascertained that the mission of the Digital and Intelligence Service includes defending the country's critical infrastructure.[184]

Examining Nations without a Cyber Force

In 2017, Boeke conducted a comparative analysis of the various cyber defense establishments in the Netherlands, Denmark, Estonia, and the

Czech Republic. This study examined how these nations deal with malware—including ransomware—and concluded that although each nation has organizations tasked with defending its cyberspace domains (including critical infrastructure), these groups are insufficient to counter the threats assailing their networks.[185] Additionally, the organizations defending government and private-sector systems are not the same as those protecting military networks.

In the United Kingdom, the National Cyber Security Centre (NCSC) is the primary lead for cybersecurity.[186] Directly subordinate to the Government Communications Headquarters (GCHQ), defending the U.K.'s critical infrastructure from ransomware falls within the duties of the NCSC.[187][188] However, the NCSC is a civilian agency separate from and distinct from the National Cyber Force (NCF), which is co-subordinate to the Ministry of Defence and GCHQ.[189] The NCF is a hybrid military/intelligence organization.[190] While the NCSC styles itself as a defensive organization, the NCF takes an offensive posture to combat threats.[191][192] The research by Devanny et al. found evidence of internal divisiveness stemming from the dual parent organization, leading to competing priorities within the cyber organization.[193]

Canada also faces increasing ransomware attacks targeting its critical national infrastructure.[194] The Centre for Cyber Security defends Canada's critical infrastructure from ransomware attacks.[195] However, this organization is unaffiliated with the Canadian military. Instead, the Centre for Cyber Security is a component of the civilian Communications Security Establishment.[196]

Organization of Current Cyber Defenses in the United States

The 2018 U.S. National Cyber Strategy highlights four pillars, each corresponding to one within the National Security Strategy.[197] The first pillar, Protect the American People, the Homeland, and the American Way of Life, includes the sub-objective: Reduce Threats from Transnational Criminal Organizations in Cyberspace.[198] This sub-objective directly addresses the threat of ransomware and the challenges associated with combating it. The strategy establishes that the federal government must collaborate with state, city, tribal, and private institutions to coordinate cyberdefense of American networks.[199]

Within the United States, the Cybersecurity and Infrastructure Security Agency (CISA) "is the operational lead for federal cybersecurity and the national coordinator for critical infrastructure security and resilience."[200] It is a relatively new organization that the government formed in 2018.[201] The CISA's mission is to "lead the national effort to understand, manage, and reduce risk to our cyber and physical infrastructure."[202] In conjunction with its Mission Enabling Offices, the CISA comprises six divisions: the Cybersecurity Division, the Emergency Communications Division, the Infrastructure Security Division, the Stakeholder Engagement Division, the Integrated Operations Division, and the National Risk Management Center.[203] However, a study by Banisakher et al. noted that the role of CISA is primarily a coordinative function, as private institutions, not the federal government, control, own, and operate 85-90% of America's critical infrastructure.[204]

While the CISA may be the leading organization for cyber defense in the United States, it is far from the only government organization involved in this endeavor. The Cyber Threat Intelligence Integration Center (CTIIC) under the Office of the Director of National Intelligence (ODNI), DHS, NSA, FBI, Department of Justice (DOJ), USSS, Department of Energy (DOE), DOD, Federal Aviation Administration (FAA), Environmental Protection Agency (EPA), TREAS, NIST, National Cyber Investigative Joint Task Force (NCIJTF), the Office of the National Cyber Director (ONCD), and others all play various roles in the cyberdefense of the nation—some via direct action, while other contribute through support.[205][206][207][208][209][210][211][212] However, due to the restrictions of America's Posse Comitatus Act, military missions operate separately from those of civilian organizations—including cyber missions.[213][214] The 2018 Department of Defense (DOD) Cyber Strategy acknowledges that "the open, transnational, and decentralized nature of the Internet that [it seeks] to protect creates significant vulnerabilities."[215] However, the strategy focuses all concerns on adversarial nation-states like China and Russia. It does not address the impact that cybercriminals engaging in transnational crime could have on military networks.

The Defense Information System Agency (DISA) provides Department of Defense information network (DODIN) operations for the military, while the United States Cyber Command (USCYBERCOM) is the primary line of defense protecting DODIN systems from attacks and intrusions.[216][217] USCYBERCOM's stated mission is "to plan and execute global cyber operations, activities, and missions to defend and advance national interests in collaboration with domestic and international partners across the full spectrum of competition and conflict."[218] As such, threats such as ransomware attacks against critical infrastructure fall within USCYBERCOM's duties. USCYBERCOM recognizes ransomware as a threat to national security and works with the National Security Agency (NSA) to execute offensive cyber missions against ransomware actors.[219][220]

The federal government is cognizant that cyber threats are rapidly evolving and may soon render traditional methods of countering them inadequate. Serwin et al. observed that this knowledge spurred the United States Senate to pass the Strengthening American Cybersecurity Act of 2022 unanimously.[221] Similarly, Baldwin et al. also asserted that the dynamic nature of cyber threats forced the Senate to adopt this new act.[222] The Strengthening American Cybersecurity Act mandates that organizations report all significant cyber incidents (regardless of whether a data breach occurred) to the CISA within 72 hours, and all ransomware payments within 24 hours.[223][224]

Notions on Ransomware Interdiction

U.S. President Joe Biden has addressed the issue of ransomware in face-to-face talks with Russian President Vladimir Putin; however, he was unable to reach a resolution (or even an acknowledgment) of the problem.[225] This lack of progress is not entirely unexpected, as research indicates that although Russia exerts some sway over the activities of

Russian cybergangs, the Russian government has no direct control over their criminal activities and may not be capable of halting them, even if it were so inclined.[226227] Russia's disregard of the ransomware cybergangs may be an attempt to save face in the international community by having to publicly concede that the Russian government cannot end, or even mitigate the menace. However, the ultimate question of whether the Russian government can act to halt or reduce ransomware originating within its borders is not attracting the international community's attention. The international community regards Russia as complicit in their struggle against ransomware; as such, they have deliberately excluded Russia from their efforts to fight ransomware in all but terrorism and cyberterrorist-related affairs. [228229230] Conversely, some researchers argue that excluding Russia from international counter-ransomware efforts will unnecessarily constrain their effectiveness.[231]

Protecting critical infrastructure entails both defensive and offensive cyber operations, and some researchers assert that integrating these two mission sets into a cohesive whole is the most effective approach.[232233234235] However, as both government and non-governmental organizations own and administer the various elements of America's critical infrastructure, much debate remains over the most effective and efficient way to defend it against ransomware attacks.[236237] With this thorough understanding of ransomware's nature, the mounting threat it represents, and the shortcomings of existing countermeasures, it is now appropriate to examine prevailing theories and approaches to countering the evolving threat posed by ransomware deployed by Russian cybergangs against America's critical infrastructure. The review divides the data into three sections: defensive ransomware interdiction strategies, offensive ransomware interdiction strategies, and advocates and opponents of establishing a cyber force. As some counter-ransomware techniques developed for non-critical infrastructure systems may apply to protecting critical infrastructure, this section will also assess the different approaches.

Defensive Ransomware Interdiction Strategies

The United States has spent years developing and adjusting legislation to deter and defeat ransomware attacks; however, it has only recently shifted from a reactive to a proactive approach.[238] Aware of the current deficiencies in America's war against ransomware, on March 15, 2023, President Joe Biden signed new cybersecurity incident reporting mandates into law, requiring critical national infrastructure (CNI) administrators to notify the federal government of all cyberattacks immediately.[239] This law aligned with his declared strategy to strengthen cybersecurity in the United States and mitigate ransomware attacks. Adamov and Carlsson assessed ransomware mitigation methods. Their research found that the best nodes to focus on in mitigation are ransomware delivery methods, network traffic, payment forms, hardware and software purposed to interdict ransomware, and educated users.[240] Exploring recommendations for cybersecurity leaders, Burt-Miller ascertained that organizations could better thwart ransomware through "better comprehensive training, critical infrastructure protection re-design & strategy, and critical infrastructure investments."[241]

An alternative approach noted by Kerner[242] is for organizations to hire ethical hackers to defend networked organizational assets against malicious threats. Galinkin researched the effectiveness of four counter-ransomware strategies: reducing successful attacks, obtaining cyber insurance, deploying decrypter technologies, and using off-site backups. Of these four options, the findings indicated that off-site backups were the most effective solution.[243] These findings echo Mohammad's conclusion that redundant backups are the best protection against ransomware.[244] Conversely, another study determined that although decreasing ransomware is a real possibility, eliminating it is not.[245] As such, Ozer proposed the creation of a "global ransomware center."[246] This organization would maintain extensive databases and work with nations worldwide to combat ransomware as a unified whole.

Akinde et al. researched detection and prevention methods and concluded that users need only exercise greater caution, while information system administrators should increase the frequency of routine network scanning.[247] Conversely, Oz et al. asserted that solutions like this lack comprehensiveness and are impractical.[248] Ideally, an organization should detect ransomware the instant an attack begins; however, the rapid evolution of ransomware makes this goal infeasible.[249] Nevertheless, Kim et al. found that if data scientists can track the evolution and inception of new ransomware variants, early detection may be possible.[250] Ultimately, defensive technique conversations return to the creation of more legislation for critical infrastructure sectors in the United States.[251]

Offensive Ransomware Interdiction Strategies

President Biden has pushed for both offensive and defensive strategies against ransomware. In 2021, the Biden Administration established the International Counter-Ransomware Initiative (CRI) to collaborate with partners worldwide to combat ransomware.[252] In addition, Biden has sought to ensure that cybergangs suffer severe repercussions from their ransomware attacks. In April 2021, the Biden Administration sanctioned cybercriminals who aided the Russian government in the SolarWinds cyberattack.[253] Biden went on to publicly state that if Russia did not rein in its cybergangs attacking America, or if Russia engaged in state-connived cybercrimes, threatening American interests, the United States would retaliate in an unspecified fashion.[254]

The United States and the United Kingdom collaborated to launch an offensive against Russian cybergangs by sanctioning the Trickbot gang.[255] Keary believes the United States can use legislation as an effective offensive tool against ransomware. He asserts that continued pressure from cyber-related legislation against Russia, coupled with additional sanctions on Russia and the cryptocurrencies facilitating ransomware attacks, will eventually yield positive results in curtailing the attacks.[256]

The U.S. Global Ransomware Summit revealed that America's previous sanctions had not had a discernible impact on Russia's tacit endorsement of these cybergangs.[257] According to expert opinion, the United States should adopt a similar approach to addressing cybercriminals as it did in its response to ISIS.[258] However, this scenario may present certain complexities, as cybercriminals operate within Russia's territorial jurisdiction.[259] Additionally, the DHS is "working to expand multilateral cooperative agreements with international partners to reach cyber criminals from regions outside the United States."[260] Alternatively, Jasper[261] suggested that America could pursue cybercriminal assets or attack their infrastructure. While Comizio et al. studied the ransomware conundrum and proposed four counter-ransomware offensives: updating and clarifying anti-ransomware laws, prioritizing infrastructure counter-ransomware efforts in the private sector, increasing public transparency of counter-ransomware offensives, and reviewing options that would enable the military to provide more significant assistance to law enforcement in the pursuit of defending America's critical infrastructure.[262]

Advocates of Cyber Force Establishment

This research is not the first work to address the question of creating a cyber force. The issue has become increasingly concerning in the United States as various parties take opposing positions about a cyber force. Retired Admiral James Stavridis, former Supreme Allied Commander Europe (2009-2013), is a vocal proponent of establishing a cyber force. According to Admiral Stavridis, the size of a prospective Cyber Force would be comparatively small relative to the Space Force, with an estimated 5,000 uniformed personnel.[263] He noted that the government could nest the new military force within the DOD or the DHS.[264] Additionally, as with the Space Force, the government could integrate a Cyber Force into an existing civilian-led agency or military department, thereby minimizing additional budget costs.[265] Admiral Stavridis went on to state, "Most important, the creation of a [U.S. Cyber Force] would move America beyond the current 'pick-up team' approach to cybersecurity, wherein each of the armed forces has a small number of cyber experts."[266]

Admiral Stavridis' points present a compelling perspective; however, we should consider the DOD's existing roles and responsibilities concerning critical infrastructure. "The DOD has two roles for critical infrastructure protection, first as a Federal department and second as a Sector-Specific Agency for one of seventeen national infrastructure sectors-the Defense Industrial Base." [267] While, as a federal department, the DOD's tasks encompass the "identification, prioritization, assessment, remediation, and protection of defense critical infrastructure," this role is primarily limited to collaborating with federal, "state and local governments and the private sector to accomplish this objective."[268] These duties starkly contrast with the roles and responsibilities that Admiral Stavridis advocates, which would have the DOD take point on America's cyberdefense under the operations of a new service component.

In 2016, Major Matt Graham put forward an argument similar to Admiral Stavridis's. He insisted that the military establish an autonomous U.S. Cyber Force comparable to the Army, Navy, Air Force, and Marine Corps, with a focus on cyberspace.[269] He opined that establishing an autonomous cyber force may facilitate the requisite degree of focus on activities in cyberspace. Enhanced attention is necessary to cultivate proficiency in cyberspace across the military, with potential benefits in three key domains: fostering leadership, developing cyberwarriors, and conducting operations in cyberspace.[270]

Winn[271] contended that it is only a matter of time before the United States recognizes that a cyber force is necessary. He acknowledged that USCYBERCOM works with the NSA and the Central Security Service (CSS) to create and prepare cyber warfighters.[272] However, he noted that a "congressionally mandated Cyberspace Solarium Commission, the rapidly growing cyber mission requires ambitious government reform and reorganization that creates a nimble, less disjointed force structure that can take on more in both 'scope and scale'." [273] Additionally, Winn noted that the possibility of a cyber force finding a home beyond the Defense Department was a possibility.[274] He insisted that, in peacetime, the Department of Homeland Security could be a suitable host for a Cyber Guard, which would possess capabilities comparable to those of the Coast Guard in global security and law enforcement.[275] The government could transfer this entity to the Army or Air Force during war.[276] Burt[277] observed that the first quarter of 2023 saw numerous veterans advocating for a new cyber force to meet and counter growing cyberspace challenges. His research noted that the Military Cyber Professionals Association (MCPA) believes the United States may lose its cyberspace hegemony.[278] In addition, in the face of these rising threats, the hodgepodge USCYBERCOM will be unable to address them adequately.[279]

Evolution of Ransomware Summary

In this chapter, the researcher examined the extant literature on ransomware. The assessment commenced with an analysis of the historical use of ransom, illustrating that criminals have ransomed for hundreds of years. The author analyzed the emergence and proliferation of ransomware and examined its mechanics. Subsequently, the researcher analyzed the factors facilitating the effectiveness of ransomware attacks. The author concluded this review by evaluating the links between Russia and ransomware.

Computers are essential components of our daily routines. Specific computer systems are critical for normal operations within the nation and for maintaining national security. Countering ransomware requires a proactive rather than reactive approach. Reactive approaches will jeopardize the nation's security and create exploitable gaps in daily operations. An all-encompassing counter-ransomware strategy may not be feasible; however, implementing measures to reduce or mitigate ransomware attacks may be achievable. As such, this researcher investigated tactics to interdict ransomware assaults on industries, causing cybergangs to deem successful ransomware attacks unfeasible.

3
Research Methodology

This research examined how well various institutions in the United States contend against ransomware attacks. The compilation and analysis of data enabled the formulation of a strategy recommendation for the United States to address cyberattacks perpetrated by adversarial, non-state entities that operate under the protection of colluding nation-states.

Research Design

The central research question was: What strategies can the United States federal government adopt and implement to thwart ransomware attacks on critical infrastructures by cybercriminal gangs operating from within Russia? The research design for this project was qualitative. There are five different qualitative approaches: narrative, phenomenology, grounded theory, ethnography, and case study. Each qualitative method was analyzed to determine which was most appropriate for developing a theory to answer the central question. Researchers use grounded theory to develop a broad, conceptual theory of a process, activity, or interaction grounded in participants' viewpoints by collecting and refining interrelated data across several phases. As such, the researcher applied a qualitative, grounded theory approach to develop a theory that answered the central question.

Strategy of Inquiry

When dealing with cybercrimes, the term big game hunting (BGH) refers to the "tactic of going after high-earning organizations across industries in often sophisticated [cyberattack] campaigns [or] the process of focusing on high-value data or assets within a business."[280] Ransomware attack patterns regularly fluctuate and evolve, and multiple reports from penetration testing, information security, business intelligence, and cybersecurity companies document that, midway through 2021, most ransomware attackers began to engage in big-game-hunting-style attacks.[281][282][283][284][285] BGH ransomware attacks grew exponentially, becoming the predominant ransomware threat to large organizations.[286][287] Additionally, this period saw ransomware trends begin to shift from predominantly information encryption to a multipronged style of not only encryption but also frequently seizing data and blackmailing victims, initiating DDoS attacks, shaming organizations by threatening to release data on morally questionable activities, or even extorting clients with the data obtained during the security breach.[288]

The constant evolution of ransomware necessitates limiting this analysis to the two years from mid-2021 through mid-2023, to focus on the most recent attack patterns. The researcher collected open-source data on ransomware attacks on government and corporate institutions in the United States over 24 months, from July 2021 to July 2023. Additionally, as this research focused on preventing ransomware attacks on critical infrastructure, confining this portion to information on institutional ransomware attacks rather than attacks on private citizens is appropriate.

Existing research indicates that most successful ransomware attacks on organizations succeed because users of information systems fail to adhere to organizational security policies, creating vulnerabilities.[289][290] The researcher analyzed the collected data for correlations in ransomware attacks to assess whether cybercriminals are exploiting common vulnerabilities to target corporate, government, and military information systems. The purpose was to evaluate whether the networks of certain institutions are more resilient to ransomware attacks than others. The results of this research will enable the development of a theory on whether a single organization overseeing corporate, government, and military information systems can create and enforce security policies that diminish the effectiveness of ransomware attacks.

Sample

Institutions may be inclined not to disclose information about successful ransomware attacks, as such disclosures could negatively impact public perceptions of the institution or inspire recurrent attacks. Additionally, some organizations may classify such matters in the interests of national security. As a result, this research will focus exclusively on publicly available, unclassified official reports on ransomware attacks (open-source reports). The researcher set out to gather information on 15 institutions affected by ransomware attacks over the past two years (five corporate, five government, and five military).

Setting

This research did not require physical interaction between the researcher, the organizations from which the researcher gathered information, or the groups under analysis. As a result, the research was conducted digitally, using digital information systems (computers). The researcher recorded data in the cloud (e.g., OneDrive). Additionally, the researcher used the Microsoft note-taking app OneNote to make the required notes. The research timeframe was 24 months, from July 2021 to July 2023, with a focus exclusively on ransomware attacks targeting corporate, government, and military entities in the United States.

Instruments/Measures

The researcher sought to determine which institutions could mount the most effective defense against ransomware attacks—corporate, government, or military. To assess these elements, the researcher reviewed each sector's five most recent ransomware attacks during the analysis period to determine the institution's resilience to these cyberattacks. The instruments the researcher used were databases maintained by U.S. cybersecurity firms.

Data Collection Strategy

In this phase, the researcher gathered reports from penetration testing, information security, business intelligence, and cybersecurity companies. These reports detailed public records of cyberattacks that occurred in the United States. The researcher examined the reports for pertinent data regarding ransomware attacks against corporate, government, and military computer networks. The researcher used data from three different cybersecurity organizations to reduce the probability of error or bias.

Data Analysis Strategy

The analysis focused on which sector (corporate, government, or military) experienced the fewest successful ransomware attacks during the analysis period. The following information details the ten possible outcomes of the analysis:

Possible Outcome Descriptions	Value
• Higher in corporate environments than in government or the military	(C > G or M)
• Higher in the government than in corporate environments or the military	(G > C or M)
• Higher in the military than in corporate environments or the government	(M > C or G)
• Higher in corporate environments than in government and the military	(C > G & M)
• Higher in the government than in corporate environments and the military	(G > C & M)
• Higher in the military than in corporate environments and the government	(M > C & G)
• Higher in corporate environments and government than in the military	(C & G > M)
• Higher in corporate environments and the military than in government	(C & M > G)

- Higher in the government and the military than in corporate environments (G & M > C)

- Comparable levels across corporate, government, and military sectors (C = G = M)

Concerning the number of successful ransomware attacks each institution suffered, the responses evaluated for the first research sub-question regarding the impact of centralizing America's cyberdefense to prevent ransomware attacks were:

Sub-question #1 Potential Response Descriptions	**Value**
• It is more than likely to have a positive, beneficial impact	(Probable)
• It is likely to have a positive, beneficial impact	(Likely)
• It is less than likely to have a positive, beneficial impact	(Unlikely)
• It is unlikely to have a positive, beneficial impact	(Improbable)

The second research sub-question examined the impact of establishing a Cyber Force with a dual mission, similar to the Coast Guard's, on America's efforts to combat ransomware threats. Based on the number of successful ransomware attacks each institution experienced, the responses considered were:

Sub-question #2 Potential Response Descriptions	**Value**
• It is projected to have a very beneficial impact	(Very Beneficial)
• It is projected to have a beneficial impact	(Beneficial)

- It is projected to have a negligible impact (Negligible)
- It is projected to have a detrimental impact (Detrimental)
- It is projected to have a very detrimental (Very Detrimental)

Given the possible outcome descriptions and potential responses to the two research sub-questions, the researcher created the following list of combination variables that link outcomes to specific responses. The researcher would then match the results of the research to one of the integrated combinations to serve as an interpretation of the research, answering the main research question:

Potential Interpretations of Integrated Research Results

- (C > G or M) = Likely / Beneficial
- (G > C or M) = Unlikely / Detrimental
- (M > C or G) = Unlikely / Detrimental
- (C > G & M) = Probable / Very Beneficial
- (G > C & M) = Unlikely / Very Detrimental
- (M > C & G) = Unlikely / Very Detrimental
- (C & G > M) = Unlikely / Detrimental
- (C & M > G) = Unlikely / Detrimental
- (G & M > C) = Unlikely / Negative
- (C = G = M) = Unlikely / Negligible

Role of the Researcher

The primary duty of the researcher in this project was to maintain the research's validity by observing the most rigorous ethical standards. The responsibilities of this position involved abstaining from any endeavors to influence the research outcome in favor of a particular result. In addition, the researcher conscientiously observed and documented the methods and results of the investigation to construct a theoretical framework that focused on the research questions. The research emphasized observation and objective analysis as essential components.

Ethical Considerations

This research assumed that the Russian Federation intentionally feigns ignorance of the presence of transnational, non-state actors within its territory who engage in cybercrimes against other nation-states.[291] Russia is potentially aware of its cybergangs; however, as of this research, it has not undertaken substantial measures to address this issue. Russia continues to contest the assertions regarding the existence of cybercriminal groups. This research advanced the proposition that other sovereign states tend to overlook the existence of domestic cybercriminals who engage in activities that extend beyond national borders. Identifying and detecting these countries was considered a secondary aspect of this research, as they were not its primary focus. A noteworthy factor is the potential existence of classified information, which may hinder public access to substantial evidence.

Research Methodology Summary

The researcher thoroughly analyzed various strategies to identify the most optimal approach for mitigating ransomware infiltration into critical infrastructure within the United States by Russian cybergangs. After excluding other alternatives, case study and grounded theory remained viable options. Case studies are commonly employed as a research method to investigate and analyze a program, event, activity, process, or individual by systematically gathering and examining data over an extended period. In contrast, researchers employ grounded theory to develop a comprehensive, conceptual theory of a particular process, activity, or interaction. Deciding on a qualitative, grounded theory approach, the researcher developed an inquiry strategy to evaluate 15 ransomware attacks across different industries. The researcher determined that the five most recent ransomware attacks on corporate, government, and military networks during the research period would ensure the samples' relevance. The chapter concluded with an outline of the collection and analysis strategies, establishing the final parameters for the research.

4

Analysis of Ransomware Attacks

This research aimed to assess the feasibility of implementing commercial strategies to prevent, deter, reduce, or mitigate ransomware attacks conducted by Russian cybergangs while avoiding the risk of armed conflict with Russia. The researcher employed a qualitative research methodology to examine data on ransomware assaults to identify a viable solution to the research questions. To formulate a comprehensive strategy for the United States to efficiently counter ransomware attacks by non-state actors, with assistance from cooperating nation-states, the researcher examined ransomware incidents targeting various domestic organizations. This investigation aimed to identify the industries that have exhibited the greatest efficacy in mitigating this dangerous software.

The researcher collected data from three organizations tracking ransomware attacks: Comparitech, Cloudian, and the Center for Strategic and International Studies (CSIS). Comparitech is a company founded in 2015 that researches cybersecurity breaches, tests virtual private networks (VPNs), and analyzes the efficacy of antivirus software.[292] Founded in 2011, Cloudian is a large-scale provider of digital file storage.[293] Established in 1962, the Center for Strategic and International Studies (CSIS) is a non-profit organization that researches current and future national security matters.[294] Each of these organizations published ransomware reports covering the research period of July 2021 through July 2023.

Comparitech's Map of Worldwide Ransomware Attacks presents a graphic chart and log of reported ransomware attacks from 2018 to the present. During the period under study, Comparitech documented 1,073 ransomware attacks. Comparitech delineated organizations under attack into four categories: healthcare, education, government, and business. This research focuses on ransomware attacks against governments, businesses, and the military, so the researcher excluded attacks on healthcare and educational institutions. From July 2021 through July 2023, Comparitech recorded 642 ransomware attacks on businesses, 108 attacks against governments, and none against DODIN systems.[295]

Cloudian's Ransomware Attack List and Alerts is an ongoing log of significant ransomware events reported worldwide from January 2020 to the present. Cloudian identified 480 ransomware attacks during the specified period. Although this report did not group the attacks by organization type, Cloudian reported no ransomware attacks on DODIN systems.[296]

Rather than tracking all ransomware attacks, the CSIS Significant Cyber Incidents Since 2006 report focuses only on ransomware incidents where losses exceeded $1 million. CSIS reported 264 events worldwide during the timeframe.[297] Of the 264 verified attacks, only two affected a United States business, government, or military—one successful attack on a government institution and one success against a private company. There is no recorded evidence of successful ransomware attacks against DODIN systems.

The original aim of this research was to compare the damage caused by 15 ransomware attacks against government organizations, corporate entities, and military networks to assess how well each group withstood the attacks, with 5 attacks per group. However, as there is no evidence that Department of Defense networks suffered any successful ransomware attacks during the evaluation period, the following details only 10 ransomware attacks.

Corporate Ransomware Attack Samples:

February 2023: The LockBit ransomware gang compromised the Managed Care of North America (MCNA) Dental network.[298] The group publicly released the initial data samples that were illicitly obtained from the healthcare provider and threatened to disclose a substantial amount of sensitive and confidential data, amounting to 700GB, demanding $10 million to refrain from releasing the data.[299]

January 2023: Cybercriminals with ties to Iran conducted ransomware assaults targeting public infrastructure in the United States and private entities in Australia, successfully exfiltrating data.[300] According to Australian police, the exfiltrated data was intended for use in extortion activities.[301]

August 2022: Practice Resources, LLC officially acknowledged a data breach after a ransomware attack.[302] Based on the findings, the breach incident exposed the data belonging to 924,138 patients.[303]

May 2022: On August 10, Cisco acknowledged a security compromise on May 24.[304] The actions of the cybercriminal organization Yanluowang prompted Cisco to admit responsibility, asserting that it had acquired substantial data and released a roster of files purportedly pilfered from Cisco.[305]

February 2022: An attack on McDonald's Corporation by the Snatch ransomware organization (associated with Russia) occurred amidst concerns raised by federal officials regarding the possibility of extensive targeting of U.S. firms following Russia's aggressive invasion of Ukraine. Snatch asserted that they had acquired 500 terabytes of data.[306] The group publicized their demand for an undisclosed ransom on the dark web.[307]

Government Ransomware Attack Samples:

August 2022: The Wheat Ridge municipality, a suburb of Denver, Colorado, suffered a ransomware attack, with attackers demanding $5 million to restore access to the city's municipal services. Following the security breach, the municipal authorities deactivated their telephone and email systems to assess the situation comprehensively.[308] Consequently, the city hall was rendered inaccessible to the public for one week. Wheat Ridge had the necessary redundancy to recover effectively and declined ransom payments.[309]

April 2022: The Glenn County Office of Education in California experienced a ransomware attack that disrupted many internet-based services, including email, phone systems, and financial software.[310] The Quantum ransomware group claimed responsibility for the attack and demanded a $1 million ransom. The Glenn County Office of

Education ultimately disbursed $400,000 to the individuals responsible for the cyberattack.[311]

January 2022: The government of Bernalillo County, New Mexico, experienced a suspected ransomware attack, prompting measures such as setting affected systems to offline status, closing most county facilities to the public, and imposing a lockdown at the detention center.[312][313]

January 2022: Crawford County, Arkansas, suffered a ransomware attack targeting its servers during the Christmas period.[314] The Crawford County IT provider deactivated its systems; however, the county continued to grapple with the attack's repercussions through January 2022, resulting in difficulties executing routine county activities.[315]

December 2021: The Maryland Department of Health experienced a ransomware attack, resulting in a system outage and a reduction in available resources for its staff.[316][317]

Military Ransomware Attack Samples:

The researcher found no evidence of successful ransomware attacks on DODIN systems from July 2021 through July 2023.

Ransomware Attack Analysis Summary

The data obtained and analyzed in this chapter indicate that corporate and government networks are subject to ransomware attacks far more frequently than military networks, as both corporate and government entities experienced multiple ransomware attacks during the research period, whereas the DOD incurred none. Indeed, successful attacks against corporate and government networks numbered in the hundreds during this period. However, the researcher noted that no successful ransomware attacks have occurred against military networks. This observation does not mean no attacks against DODIN occurred during this period. There was significant evidence that bad actors launched additional cyberattacks against military networks (many of which were state-sponsored or state-directed); however, none of these attacks used ransomware. It is worth noting that even government law enforcement agencies have been victims of ransomware attacks. Moody[318] also reported that city, county, state, and even federal law enforcement agencies (e.g., the U.S. Marshals Service) have been hit by ransomware attacks during the evaluation period. Additionally, although it is evident that corporations experienced ransomware attacks at a higher rate than government organizations, both groups still suffered hundreds of successful ransomware attacks, whereas the military did not.

The following results emerged when the researcher applied this data to the research questions and possible outcomes:

Ransomware attacks were higher in corporate environments and government than in the military (C & G > M)

- *What is the impact of centralizing America's cyberdefense to thwart the spread of ransomware?*
  - It is more than likely to have a positive, beneficial impact (Probable)
- *What kind of impact would creating a Cyber Force with a dual mission analogous to the Coast Guard's dual missions have on America's goal of countering ransomware threats?*
  - It is projected to have a very beneficial impact (Very Beneficial)

Research indicates that the U.S. federal government could create a Cyber Force with a dual mission, analogous to the Coast Guard's, to centralize America's cyberdefenses and thwart ransomware attacks on critical infrastructure by cybercriminal gangs operating from within Russia.

5
Policy Implications

Cybercrime poses a challenge worldwide. As integrated computer networks become increasingly embedded in our daily routines, so too does the risk of cybercrime. Ransomware is a particularly threatening form of cybercrime, as it denies users access to data and information systems and compels them to pay a ransom to regain access to their systems. In the physical world, it is akin to someone changing the locks on a home and refusing to give the owner a key until they pay the desired amount. These crimes pose a minimal threat of capture to the criminals while allowing them to generate a sizable source of illicit revenue. Ransomware is recognized as a national security threat.[319] A threat grows in scope and severity.[320] Most ransomware attacks targeting American computers originate with cybergangs operating within the Russian Federation.[321]

Historically, ransom has proven an effective means of generating profit from criminal activity. From antiquity to the modern day, criminals have used ransomware against victims.[322][323] While many people think of kidnapping when broaching the subject of ransom, the term also applies to property stolen in exchange for money. This activity also has historical precedence. However, unlike in ancient times, ransomware targets property exclusively, allowing criminals to seize control of the property without ever being in the same location as the property they have taken. This lack of collocation drastically reduces the chances that anyone will catch the criminal in the act. Additionally, because criminals typically demand ransomware payments in encrypted digital currencies, such as Bitcoin, the likelihood of apprehending the perpetrator drops even further.

This low risk has made ransomware attractive to cybercriminals operating in remote locations, such as the Russian Federation. Many users find that they possess limited options in recovering access or control over the compromised computers, and as a result, many victims choose to pay, and the cybergangs abscond with their money unfettered. Further complicating matters, Russian cybergangs often use botnets to distribute ransomware attacks across cyberspace en masse, resulting in a system that generates enormous profits for little risk. The increasing effectiveness and profitability of ransomware attacks spur cybercriminals to pursue subsequent attacks, thereby expanding their illicit operations. The rising frequency of these ransomware attacks provoked the American government to designate this malicious software as a national security threat.[324]

Cyberattack records indicate that private-sector and government information systems are vulnerable to ransomware attacks, with multiple incidents occurring each month, including some targeting law enforcement agencies.[325] History also shows that even information systems supporting national critical infrastructure are susceptible to ransomware attacks, highlighting the extreme dangers of this malware.[326] Non-state actors and bad actors in Russia can constrain and disrupt the functions of critical infrastructure within the nation—this undesirable situation merits government action to address it. This research aimed to analyze procedures to halt or significantly reduce ransomware attacks carried out by Russian cybercriminals without risking military conflict with the Russian Federation.

To accomplish this goal, the researcher conducted a qualitative analysis to assess strategies the United States federal government could adopt and implement to thwart ransomware attacks on critical infrastructures by cybercriminal gangs operating from within Russia. The two specific research questions analyzed were: What is the impact of centralizing America's cyberdefense to thwart the spread of ransomware? What kind of impact would creating a Cyber Force with a dual mission analogous to the Coast Guard's dual missions have on America's goal of countering ransomware threats? The researcher collected data from 15 organizations that experienced ransomware attacks over the last two years (five corporate, five government, and five military) to determine whether a single entity can establish and implement security standards across corporate, government, and military information systems to reduce the effectiveness of ransomware attacks.

The researcher anticipated that there would be records of each group suffering ransomware attacks over the 24 months analyzed. However, while corporate and government networks experienced multiple ransomware attacks over the two years, no Department of Defense information systems fell victim to ransomware. Yes, the military did endure cyberattacks in the 24 months the researcher reviewed. However, none of those cyberattacks were ransomware incidents. The reason for the lack of ransomware attacks on the military networks remains unknown.

Implications

The lack of successful ransomware attacks on DODIN non-classified internet protocol router networks (NIPRNet) systems implies that DISA and USCYBERCOM have fortified DODIN systems to inhibit successful ransomware attacks in a manner superior to the network standards applied in corporate and government information system environments.

Conclusions on Policy Implications

Given the research results, the researcher concludes that centralizing America's cyberdefense to thwart the spread of ransomware would have a positive impact. Additionally, as the DOD has prevented any ransomware attacks while corporate and government networks have not, the researcher concludes that creating a Cyber Force to defend and administrate networks in America, supporting the nation's critical infrastructure, would also benefit the country's information security. The framework, organizational structure, and daily operations of such an organization would depend on the status of current network infrastructure, the functions each component provides to support the nation, federal budgetary allotments, and the legal limitations of the United States. Thus, the researcher concludes that creating a Cyber Force is an effective strategy that the United States federal government can adopt and implement to thwart ransomware attacks on critical infrastructures by cybercriminal gangs operating from within Russia.

Policy Recommendations

According to the U.S. Senate Committee on Commerce, Science, and Transportation,[327] Russian cybercriminals have advanced ransomware to a level that could cause severe damage to essential sectors of the country. Mitigating this emergent menace necessitates that America take action to remediate the problem—action grounded in analytical examinations and methodical research into the nature of the issue. The implications and conclusions of this research are significant because they will enable researchers, security practitioners, and policymakers to make informed decisions about the best courses of action.

Advice to Practitioners

Security practitioners should note that, despite thousands of online information systems, the Department of Defense avoided ransomware attacks over the 24 months analyzed in this research. In contrast, those in corporate America and the government were victims of multiple attacks. Protecting information systems across the digital domain is an arduous task. However, security practitioners tasked with defending corporate and government networked systems against ransomware threats should review military applications of DODIN security to protect better the information systems they are responsible for shielding.

Advice to Policymakers

Ransomware's threat to national security is increasing annually.[328] Combating this threat requires a proactive stance by those in positions to affect policies regarding cyberspace across American networks. Although creating and integrating another government agency is cumbersome, policymakers should consider creating a cyber force to defend and administer the integrity of American networks. Existing services merely monitor and advise on cybersecurity matters; however, a new agency with the power and authority to protect and manage network operations at the level affected by the DOD will fortify networks in the United States to the extent that ransomware attacks become less effective. As a profit-driven crime, the lack of successful ransomware incidents should lead to a cessation or a drastic reduction in ransomware incursions by Russian cybergangs, without risking a military confrontation with Russia.

Advice to Researchers

This research was limited to addressing the specific Russian cybergang ransomware threat against American critical infrastructure systems. Through this research, the author proposed that establishing a Cyber Force would effectively counter the ransomware threat posed by cybergangs operating within the Russian Federation. Although this research establishes that military networks are generally far more resistant to ransomware attacks than those in corporate environments and government organizations, it does not explain why Defense Department information systems fare better against ransomware. There are many possibilities that might cause this phenomenon. Could it be the training that information system users receive from the DOD? Is it possible that this results from the security regulations implemented and enforced by military network administrators? Could it be the firewalls and traffic filtering applied by the Department of Defense? It could be a combination of these factors, or it may be attributable to something entirely different. The research results indicate that a Cyber Force may be beneficial for countering ransomware; however, this does not imply that it is the only—or even the most effective—strategy to achieve this goal.

It is essential to understand the cause-and-effect relationships between Russian cybergangs' prolific ransomware campaigns and the lack of successful attacks on Defense Department networks. Understanding this dynamic is critical to leveraging the military's defenses. As such, researchers should consider exploring the mechanisms allowing the Defense Information Systems Agency to protect the Department of Defense Information Systems Network.

Future researchers should explore the theory that a Cyber Force could adequately defend America's critical infrastructure from Russian ransomware attacks. Additionally, they should examine how well such a service component could withstand other forms of cyberattacks, including attacks by non-state actors in other countries and by adversarial nation-states. These analyses will facilitate further development of this theory to determine better the benefits and drawbacks of creating a Cyber Force.

Summary

As we move into the 21st Century, networked information systems have become increasingly indispensable to everyday life. Although we may not be consciously aware of their presence or operation, these systems support critical infrastructure nodes across the country. Support from these information systems will continue to increase as society progresses. This dependence on these networked systems means that America must take steps to ensure their protection, integrity, and security commensurate with their burgeoning importance and criticality.

History illustrates that criminals will often employ ransom as a profitable crime. Criminals take or deny access to people or objects of value and refuse to return the appropriated items until they receive a monetary sum in exchange. This tactic has proven successful since antiquity, with people as objects of high value often targeted for seizure. The escalating importance of networked information systems has made them attractive targets for ransomware attacks. However, another factor in ransom events is the vulnerability of the targeted objects. For example, the president of the United States would be an invaluable ransom; however, the security surrounding the president would make successfully kidnapping that individual a near impossibility. Thus, it is impractical to attempt to ransom the president. In contrast, when objects of value lack sufficient security measures, criminals perceive them as vulnerable—making them ideal targets for ransom attacks.

Cybercriminals perceive America's networked critical infrastructure information systems as vulnerable, high-value targets. As long as they view them as both vulnerable and profitable, ransomware attacks will continue. Since the value of these systems is increasing rather than decreasing, the most effective way to deter ransom events is to increase the security measures protecting them from attack. Research shows that the Department of Defense is highly effective at protecting its information systems against ransomware attacks. Consequently, a logical conclusion is that a properly structured and supplied Cyber Force may extend similar protection to all information systems supporting critical infrastructure nodes throughout the United States. Thus, creating a Cyber Force might be an effective deterrent to halt or significantly decrease ransomware attacks by Russian cybercriminal groups without incurring the risk of armed conflict with Russia.

However, ransomware is only one issue among many cyber-related challenges facing the United States—viruses, worms, DDoS attacks, phishing, social engineering, and other cyberattacks pose additional threats to American critical infrastructure. There is no evidence that a Cyber Force would provide any benefit against such threats. Additionally, the research did not address state actors. Nation-states such as China, North Korea, and Iran already engage in affairs such as cyber corporate espionage, and they are steadily refining their capabilities. The American government should exercise much caution when broaching the subject of creating a Cyber Force. Researchers and policymakers should thoroughly analyze the second, third, and fourth-order effects of creating a Cyber Force to ensure that, in the course of applying a Cyber Force solution to the ransomware problem, the United States does not inadvertently create additional, subsequent problems with the potential of inflicting more harm on the nation than the scourge of ransomware. As there is no evidence indicating that a Cyber Force would be able to create a framework to effectively and efficiently provide a defense for the nation's critical infrastructure cyber domain (without unduly consuming egregious levels of workforce, funding, and resources), this researcher would not recommend the creation of such a cyber force.

Notes

1. Columbus, "Ransomware Attacks Are Getting More Complex and Even Harder to Prevent," 2021.
2. Thomas, "Cybercrime: It's Worse Than We Thought," 2021.
3. Department of State, "Cybercrime," 2022.
4. Tidy, "US Companies Hit by 'Colossal' Cyber-attack," 2021.
5. Radauskas, "Russia Wants to Legalize Cybercrime for Homeland," 2023.
6. Shinkman, "Russia Denies Involvement in Darkside Attack on Colonial Pipeline," 2021.
7. U.S. Senate Committee on Commerce, Science, and Transportation, "Chair Cantwell on Cyber Threats to Energy Infrastructure: Colonial Pipeline Attack 'The Tip of the Iceberg'," 2021.
8. Presidential Policy Directive 21, "Critical Infrastructure Security and Resilience," 2013.
9. Cybersecurity and Infrastructure Security Agency, Energy Sector, n.d.-b.
10. Presidential Policy Directive 21, "Critical Infrastructure Security and Resilience," 2013.
11. O'Gorman and McDonald, "Ransomware: A Growing Menace," 2012.
12. Department of the Treasury, "Ransomware Trends in Bank Secrecy Act Data Between July 2021 and December 2021: Russia-Related Malware Dominates Ransomware Landscape," 2021.
13. Newman, "Russia's Sway Over Criminal Ransomware Gangs is Coming Into Focus," 2022.
14. The White House, Office of the Press Secretary, "Fact sheet: Ongoing public U.S. Efforts to Counter Ransomware," 2021.
15. Lyngaas, "Microsoft Blames Russian Military-Linked Hackers for Ransomware Attacks in Poland and Ukraine," 2022.
16. Aurangzeb et al., "Ransomware: A Survey and Trends," 2017.
17. Anstett et al., "Ransomware Attacks on Critical Infrastructure Sectors," 2022.
18. IBM, "Ransomware Persisted Despite Improved Detection in 2022," 2023.
19. Cybersecurity and Infrastructure Security Agency, "CISA Establishes Ransomware Vulnerability Warning Pilot Program," 2023.

20. Department of the Treasury, "Ransomware Trends in Bank Secrecy Act Data Between July 2021 and December 2021: Russia-Related Malware Dominates Ransomware Landscape," 2021.
21. Federal Bureau of Investigation, "Director Christopher Wray Announces Actions to Disrupt and Prosecute Russian Criminal Activity," 2022.
22. The White House, Office of the Press Secretary, "Fact Sheet: Biden-Harris Administration Announces National Cybersecurity Strategy," 2023.
23. United States Senate Committee on Commerce, Science, and Transportation, "Chair Cantwell on Cyber Threats to Energy Infrastructure: Colonial Pipeline Attack 'The Tip of the Iceberg'," 2021.
24. Shinkman, "Russia Denies Involvement in Darkside Attack on Colonial Pipeline," 2021.
25. O'Sullivan, "Cybercrime in the Gaming Sector is Up 167% Year-on-Year," 2022.
26. Swinhoe, "Why businesses don't report cybercrimes to law enforcement," 2019.
27. Center for Strategic and International Studies. "Significant Cyber Incidents." n.d.
28. Center for Strategic and International Studies. "Significant Cyber Incidents." n.d.
29. Center for Strategic and International Studies. "Significant Cyber Incidents." n.d.
30. United States Senate Committee on Commerce, Science, and Transportation, "Chair Cantwell on Cyber Threats to Energy Infrastructure: Colonial Pipeline Attack 'The Tip of the Iceberg'," 2021.
31. Nast, "Russia's Sway Over Criminal Ransomware Gangs is Coming Into Focus," 2022.
32. Department of Defense, "DOD Dictionary of Military and Associated Terms," 2021.
33. Department of Defense, "DOD Dictionary of Military and Associated Terms," 2021.
34. Department of Defense, "DOD Dictionary of Military and Associated Terms," 2021.
35. Merriam-Webster, "Definition of Cybercriminal," n.d.-a.
36. Department of Defense, "DOD Dictionary of Military and Associated Terms," 2021.

37. Department of Defense, "DOD Dictionary of Military and Associated Terms," 2021.

38. Merriam-Webster, Definition of Cyberterrorism," n.d.-b.

39. Singer and Friedman, "Cybersecurity: What Everyone Needs to Know," 2014.

40. United States Secret Service, "Preparing for a Cyber Incident: A Guide to Ransomware," n.d.-b.

41. Merriam-Webster, "Definition of Ransomware," n.d.-c.

42. National Institute of Standards and Technology, "Cybersecurity," 2023.

43. United States Air Force, "75th SFS Force Protection," n.d.

44. Federal Bureau of Investigation, "Terrorism," 2016.

45. Merriam-Webster, "Definition of Ransom," n.d.-d.

46. Cambridge Dictionary, "Ransom," n.d.

47. Merriam-Webster, "Definition of Ransomware," n.d.-c.

48. Cambridge Dictionary, "Ransom," n.d.

49. Merriam-Webster, "Definition of Ransomware," n.d.-c.

50. Encyclopedia Britannica, "The Time Julius Caesar was Captured by Pirates," 2019.

51. Marks, G., "That Time Julius Caesar was Kidnapped and Insisted His Captors Increase Their Ransom," 2021.

52. Lennox-Gentle, "Piracy, Sea Robbery, and Terrorism: Enforcing Laws to Deter Ransom Payments and Hijacking," 2010.

53. Testament Press, "Ancient Money Calculator," n.d.

54. Lennox-Gentle, "Piracy, Sea Robbery, and Terrorism: Enforcing Laws to Deter Ransom Payments and Hijacking," 2010.

55. Lennox-Gentle, "Piracy, Sea Robbery, and Terrorism: Enforcing Laws to Deter Ransom Payments and Hijacking," 2010.

56. Fremont-Barnes, "The Wars of the Barbary Pirates: To the Shores of Tripoli: The Rise of the US Navy and Marines," 2014.

57. Ambrus, Chaney, and Salitskiy, "Pirates of the Mediterranean: An Empirical Investigation of Bargaining with Asymmetric Information," 2018.

58. Constitutional Rights Foundation, "The United States and the Barbary Pirates," n.d.

59. Constitutional Rights Foundation, "The United States and the Barbary Pirates," n.d.
60. Constitutional Rights Foundation, "The United States and the Barbary Pirates," n.d.
61. Hagen, "The Story Behind the First Ransom Note in American History," 2013.
62. Hagen, "The Story Behind the First Ransom Note in American History," 2013.
63. Hagen, "The Story Behind the First Ransom Note in American History," 2013.
64. Hagen, "The Story Behind the First Ransom Note in American History," 2013.
65. Hagen, "The Story Behind the First Ransom Note in American History," 2013.
66. Hagen, "The Story Behind the First Ransom Note in American History," 2013.
67. Detotto, McCannon, and Vannini, "Understanding Ransom Kidnappings and Their Duration," 2014.
68. Detotto, McCannon, and Vannini, "Understanding Ransom Kidnappings and Their Duration," 2014.
69. Detotto, McCannon, and Vannini, "Understanding Ransom Kidnappings and Their Duration," 2014.

70 Jenkins, "Does the U.S. No-Concessions Policy Deter Kidnappings of Americans?" 2018.

71. Jenkins, "Does the U.S. No-Concessions Policy Deter Kidnappings of Americans?" 2018.
72. Jenkins, "Does the U.S. No-Concessions Policy Deter Kidnappings of Americans?" 2018.
73. Shortland and Keatinge, "Closing the Gap: Assessing Responses to Terrorist-Related Kidnap-for-Ransom," 2017.
74. Shortland and Keatinge, "Closing the Gap: Assessing Responses to Terrorist-Related Kidnap-for-Ransom," 2017.
75. Shortland and Keatinge, "Closing the Gap: Assessing Responses to Terrorist-Related Kidnap-for-Ransom," 2017.
76. Pearl, "Where Exactly is the Rule that Says Governments Can't Negotiate with Terrorists?" 2015.
77. Pearl, "Where Exactly is the Rule that Says Governments Can't Negotiate with Terrorists?" 2015.
78. Pearl, "Where Exactly is the Rule that Says Governments Can't Negotiate with Terrorists?" 2015.

79. Jenkins, "Why the U.S. swaps prisoners but doesn't pay ransom," 2014.
80. Jenkins, "Why the U.S. swaps prisoners but doesn't pay ransom," 2014.
81. Jenkins, "Why the U.S. swaps prisoners but doesn't pay ransom," 2014.
82. Dutton, "Funding Terrorism: The Problem of Ransom Payments," 2019.
83. Dutton, "Funding Terrorism: The Problem of Ransom Payments," 2019.
84. Meyer, "Why the G8 Pact to Stop Paying Terrorist Ransoms Probably Won't Work—And Isn't Even Such a Great Idea," 2013.
85. Meyer, "Why the G8 Pact to Stop Paying Terrorist Ransoms Probably Won't Work—And Isn't Even Such a Great Idea," 2013.
86. Meyer, "Why the G8 Pact to Stop Paying Terrorist Ransoms Probably Won't Work—And Isn't Even Such a Great Idea," 2013.
87. Meyer, "Why the G8 Pact to Stop Paying Terrorist Ransoms Probably Won't Work—And Isn't Even Such a Great Idea," 2013.
88. Callimachi, "Paying Ransoms, Europe Bankrolls Qaeda Terror," 2014.
89. Callimachi, "Paying Ransoms, Europe Bankrolls Qaeda Terror," 2014.
90. McGrath, "These are the Countries that Have (Probably) Paid Hostage Ransom to the Islamic State," 2015.
91. CrowdStrike, A Brief History of Ransomware [Including Attacks], 2022.
92. CrowdStrike, A Brief History of Ransomware [Including Attacks], 2022.
93. History of Information, "Dr. Joseph Popp Writes the AIDS Trojan Horse, the First Known Ransomware Cyber Attack," n.d.
94. Norton LifeLock, "When Were Computer Viruses First Written, and What Were Their Original Purposes?" n.d.
95. Sears, "Ransomware: A Bibliometric Research Study," 2021.
96. Norton LifeLock, "When Were Computer Viruses First Written, and What Were Their Original Purposes?" n.d.
97. Mat et al., "Towards a Systematic Description of the Field Using Bibliometric Analysis: Malware Evolution," 2021.
98. Mat et al., "Towards a Systematic Description of the Field Using Bibliometric Analysis: Malware Evolution," 2021.
99. Buchanan, Cyber-Attacks to Industrial Control Systems Since Stuxnet: A Systematic Review, 2022.

100. Buchanan, Cyber-Attacks to Industrial Control Systems Since Stuxnet: A Systematic Review, 2022.
101. Richardson et al., "Ransomware: The Landscape is Shifting-a Concise Report," 2021.
102. Richardson et al., "Ransomware: The Landscape is Shifting-a Concise Report," 2021.
103. Richardson et al., "Ransomware: The Landscape is Shifting-a Concise Report," 2021.
104. Swasey, "Insufficient Healthcare Cybersecurity Invites Ransomware Attacks and Sale of Phi on the Dark Web," 2020.
105. Swasey, "Insufficient Healthcare Cybersecurity Invites Ransomware Attacks and Sale of Phi on the Dark Web," 2020.
106. Williams, "Conti Ransomware Gang: An Analysis of the Group's Motives and Methods," 2022.
107. Williams, "Conti Ransomware Gang: An Analysis of the Group's Motives and Methods," 2022.
108. Holt et al., "Examining the Social Networks of Malware Writers and Hackers," 2012.
109. Holt et al., "Examining the Social Networks of Malware Writers and Hackers," 2012.
110. Nershi and Grossman, "Assessing the Political Motivations Behind Ransomware Attacks," 2022.
111. Weber, "Financial Incentives May Explain the Perceived Lack of Ransomware in Russia's Latest Assault on Ukraine," 2022.
112. Richardson, North, and Garofalo, "Ransomware: The Landscape is Shifting-a Concise Report," 2021.
113. Richardson, North, and Garofalo, "Ransomware: The Landscape is Shifting-a Concise Report," 2021.
114. Richardson, North, and Garofalo, "Ransomware: The Landscape is Shifting-a Concise Report," 2021.
115. Richardson, North, and Garofalo, "Ransomware: The Landscape is Shifting-a Concise Report," 2021.
116. Richardson, North, and Garofalo, "Ransomware: The Landscape is Shifting-a Concise Report," 2021.

117. Muslim et al., "A Study of Ransomware Attacks Evolution and Prevention," 2019.
118. Fernando, Komninos, and Chen, "A Study on the Evolution of Ransomware Detection Using Machine Learning and Deep Learning Techniques," 2020.
119. Fernando, Komninos, and Chen, "A Study on the Evolution of Ransomware Detection Using Machine Learning and Deep Learning Techniques," 2020.
120. Fernando, Komninos, and Chen, "A Study on the Evolution of Ransomware Detection Using Machine Learning and Deep Learning Techniques," 2020.
121. Wadkar, Di Troia, and Stamp, "Detecting Malware Evolution Using Support Vector Machines," 2020.
122. Alenezi et al., "Evolution of Malware Threats and Techniques: A Review," 2022.
123. Alenezi et al., "Evolution of Malware Threats and Techniques: A Review," 2022.
124. Sahay et al., "Evolution of Malware and its Detection Techniques," 2019.
125. Sahay et al., "Evolution of Malware and its Detection Techniques," 2019.
126. Tupadha and Stamp, "Machine Learning for Malware Evolution Detection," 2021.
127. Tupadha and Stamp, "Machine Learning for Malware Evolution Detection," 2021.
128. Zimba and Chishimba, "Understanding the Evolution of Ransomware: Paradigm Shifts in Attack Structures," 2019.
129. Merriam-Webster, "Definition of Ransomware," n.d.-c.
130. United States Secret Service, "Preparing for a Cyber Incident," n.d.-g.
131. United States Secret Service, "Preparing for a Cyber Incident: Contacting Law Enforcement," n.d.-e.
132. United States Secret Service, "Preparing for a Cyber Incident: Anatomy of a Business Email Compromise," n.d. d.
133. United States Secret Service, "Preparing for a Cyber Incident: An Introductory Guide," n.d.-c.
134. United States Secret Service, "Preparing for a Cyber Incident: Contacting Law Enforcement," n.d.-e.
135. United States Secret Service. "Preparing for a Cyber Incident: A Guide to Ransomware," n.d.-b.

136. United States Secret Service, "Preparing for a Cyber Incident," n.d.-g.
137. Anghel and Racautanu, "A Note on Different Types of Ransomware Attacks," 2019.
138. Hull, John, and Arief, "Ransomware Deployment Methods and Analysis: Views from a Predictive Model and Human Responses," 2019.
139. Hull, John, and Arief, "Ransomware Deployment Methods and Analysis: Views from a Predictive Model and Human Responses," 2019.
140. ARMA International, "Most Ransomware Attacks Bypass E-mail Filtering," n.d.
141. Custers, Oerlemans, and Pool, "Laundering the Profits of Ransomware: Money Laundering Methods for Vouchers and Cryptocurrencies," 2020.
142. Custers, Oerlemans, and Pool, "Laundering the Profits of Ransomware: Money Laundering Methods for Vouchers and Cryptocurrencies," 2020.
143. Hernandez-Castro, Cartwright, and Stepanova, "Economic Analysis of Ransomware," 2017.
144. O'Gorman and McDonald, "Ransomware: A Growing Menace," 2012.
145. O'Gorman and McDonald, "Ransomware: A Growing Menace," 2012.
146. O'Gorman and McDonald, "Ransomware: A Growing Menace," 2012.
147. Hunter, "'til the Next Zero-Day Comes," 2022.
148. Hunter, "'til the Next Zero-Day Comes," 2022.
149. Sabin, "Colonial Pipeline Ransomware Attack's Unexpected Legacy," 2023.
150. Novak, "Ransomware Attack on Dallas Disrupts 911, Court and Water Systems," 2023.
151. Scroxton, "Boardroom Does Not See Ransomware as a Priority," 2022.
152. Polikarpov, Eskov, and Anisimov, "Trends of Malware Influence on the Integrated IT Security Systems at Critical Infrastructure Objects," 2019.
153. Polikarpov, Eskov, and Anisimov, "Trends of Malware Influence on the Integrated IT Security Systems at Critical Infrastructure Objects," 2019.
154. Afianian et al., "Malware Dynamic Analysis Evasion Techniques: A Survey," 2019.
155. Nelson and Simek, "Ransomware: How Many Bitcoins Are in Your Wallet," 2018.
156. The Biden Administration Cracks Down on Ransomware, "American Journal of International Law, 116(2)," 2022.

157. Stent, "The great cyber game," 2018.
158. Heaven, "Can You Spot the Cryptocrime in This Picture?" 2018.
159. Financial Crimes Enforcement Network, "Financial Trend Analysis: Ransomware Trends in Bank Secrecy Act Data Between January 2021 and June 2021," 2021.
160. Dudley, "The Extortion Economy: How Insurance Companies are Fueling a Rise in Ransomware Attacks," 2019.
161. Macaulay, "The danger of critical infrastructure interdependency," 2019.
162. Macaulay, "The danger of critical infrastructure interdependency," 2019.
163. Kyung-shick, Scott, and LeClair, "Ransomware Against Police: Diagnosis of Risk Factors Via Application of Cyber-Routine Activities Theory," 2016.
164. Ryan et al., "Insecure Software on a Fragmenting Internet," 2022.
165. Ryan et al., "Insecure Software on a Fragmenting Internet," 2022.
166. Jasper, "Restraining Russian Ransomware," 2022.
167. Abely, "Ransomware, Cyber Sanctions, and the Problem of Timing," 2022.
168. Jasper, "Restraining Russian Ransomware," 2022.
169. Nast, "Russia's Ransomware Gangs are Being Named and Shamed," 2023.
170. Bushwick, "FBI Takes Down Hive Criminal Ransomware Group," 2023.
171. McLaughlin, "FBI Says it 'Hacked the Hackers' to Shut Down Major Ransomware Group," 2023.
172. Nast, "Russia's Ransomware Gangs are Being Named and Shamed," 2023.
173. Tidy, "Seven Russians Sanctioned Over Ransomware Cyber-Crime," 2023.
174. Uberti, "Russia-Linked Ransomware Groups Are Changing Tactics to Dodge Crackdowns," 2022.
175. Nast, "Russia's Sway Over Criminal Ransomware Gangs is Coming Into Focus," 2022.
176. Jasper, "Restraining Russian Ransomware," 2022.
177. United Nations, "About Us," n.d.
178. Blessing, "The Diffusion of Cyber Forces: Military Innovation and the Dynamic Implementation of Cyber Force Structure," 2020.
179. Costello and McReynolds, "China's Strategic Support Force: A Force for a New Era," 2018.

180. Costello and McReynolds, "China's Strategic Support Force: A Force for a New Era," 2018.
181. Leinhos, "Cyber Defence in Germany: Challenges and the Way Forward for the Bundeswehr," 2020.
182. Leinhos, "Cyber Defence in Germany: Challenges and the Way Forward for the Bundeswehr," 2020.
183. Aigner et al., "Singapore's Journey as a Digit-all-ized and Innovative Smart Nation Toward Sustainability," 2022.
184. Matthews and Timur, "Singapore's 'Total Defence' Strategy," 2023.
185. Boeke, "National Cyber Crisis Management: Different European Approaches," 2017.
186. Stoddart, "UK Cyber Security and Critical National Infrastructure Protection," 2016.
187. National Cyber Security Centre, "What We Do," n.d.
188. Stoddart, "UK Cyber Security and Critical National Infrastructure Protection," 2016.
189. Sengupta, "UK is About to Launch Force to Hit Hostile Countries with Cyberattacks," 2020.
190. Devanny et al., "The National Cybercforce that Britain Needs?" 2021.
191. Sengupta, "UK is About to Launch Force to Hit Hostile Countries with Cyberattacks," 2020.
192. Warrell, "GCHQ to Use New Cyber Force to Hunt Ransomware Gangs," 2021.
193. Devanny et al., "The National Cybercforce that Britain Needs?" 2021.
194. Al Jazeera, "Global Ransomware Attacks Rise 151%: Canada Spy Agency," 2021.
195. Canada.ca, "Canadian Centre for Cyber Security," 2018.
196. Canada.ca, "Canadian Centre for Cyber Security," 2023.
197. The White House "National Cyber Strategy of the United States of America," 2018.
198. The White House "National Cyber Strategy of the United States of America," 2018.
199. The White House "National Cyber Strategy of the United States of America," 2018.

200. Cybersecurity and Infrastructure Security Agency, "About CISA," n.d.-a.
201. Cybersecurity and Infrastructure Security Agency Act of 2018, Pub. L. No. 115-278, 2018.
202. Cybersecurity and Infrastructure Security Agency, "About CISA," n.d.-a.
203. Cybersecurity and Infrastructure Security Agency, "About CISA," n.d.-a.
204. Banisakher et al., "Critical Infrastructure - Perspectives on the Role of Government in Cybersecurity," 2019.
205. Department of Homeland Security, "Cybersecurity," 2023.
206. Federal Bureau of Investigation, "National Cyber Investigative Joint Task Force," n.d.
207. National Institute of Standards and Technology, "Cybersecurity," 2023.
208. National Security Agency, "Cybersecurity," n.d.
209. Office of the National Cyber Director, Office of Strategic Communications, "Cyber Threat Intelligence Integration Center Home," n.d.
210. United States Secret Service, "Cyber Investigations" n.d.
211. The White House, "National Cyber Strategy March 2023," 2023.
212. The White House, "Office of the National Cyber Director," 2024.
213. Moore, "Posse Comitatus Revisited: The Use of the Military in Civil Law Enforcement," 1987.
214. Nunn, "The Posse Comitatus Act Explained," 2021.
215. Department of Defense, "Department of Defense Cyber Strategy 2018," 2018.
216. Defense Information System Agency, "About DISA," n.d.
217. United States Cyber Command Public Affairs Office, "Cyber 101 - U.S. Cyber Command Mission," 2022.
218. United States Cyber Command Public Affairs Office, "Cyber 101 - U.S. Cyber Command Mission," 2022.
219. United States Cyber Command Public Affairs Office, "Cyber 101 - U.S. Cyber Command Mission," 2022.
220. Vaczi and Szadeczky, "A Threat for the Trains: Ransomware as a New Risk," 2019.
221. Serwin et al., "US Senate Unanimously Passes the Strengthening American Cybersecurity Act," 2022.

222. Baldwin et al., "Congress Passes New Cyber Incident and Ransomware Payment Reporting Legislation," 2022.
223. Serwin et al., "US Senate Unanimously Passes the Strengthening American Cybersecurity Act," 2022.
224. Strengthening American Cybersecurity Act of 2022, S.3600, 117th Cong., 2022.
225. Keith, "Biden and Putin Say Their Summit was Constructive as the World Waits for Results," 2021.
226. Barnes, "Russia Influences Hackers But Stops Short of Directing Them, Report Says," 2021.
227. Insikt Group, "Dark Covenant: Connections Between the Russian | Recorded Future State and Criminal Actors," 2021.
228. Sanger, "U.S. Holds Global Meeting to Fight Ransomware, Minus the World's No. 1 Culprit," 2021.
229. United Nations Security Council Counter-Terrorism Committee Executive Directorate and United Nations Office of Counter-Terrorism, "The Protection of Critical Infrastructures Against Terrorist Attacks: Compendium of Good Practices," 2018.
230. "United States Joins with Allies, Including NATO, to Attribute Malicious Cyber Activities to China," 2021.
231. Baram, "US Global Ransomware Summit: More Needs to be Done," 2021.
232. Carmack, "For Cybersecurity, the Best Defense is a Good Offense," 2021.
233. Epps, "Offensive Cyber Operations Reshaping the Modern Battlespace," 2021.
234. Pendino, Jahn, and Pedersen, "U.S. Cyber Deterrence: Bringing Offensive Capabilities Into the Light," 2022.
235. Tate and Bates, "Deterrence Thru Transparent Offensive Cyber Persistence," 2022.
236. Sanger, "U.S. Holds Global Meeting to Fight Ransomware, Minus the World's No. 1 Culprit," 2021.
237. Shull and Hilt, "Securing Cyberspace in an Age of Disruption: A Glimpse at the Rising Threatscape," 2021.
238. Ford, "Cyber Ransom in the Information Age: A Call to Arms Against the Hackers," 2021.
239. Scroxton, "Boardroom Does Not See Ransomware as a Priority," 2022.

240. Adamov and Carlsson, "The State of Ransomware. Trends and Mitigation Techniques," 2017.

241. Burt-Miller, "Exploring Cybersecurity Expert Recommendations to Fortify U.S. National Security: A Generic Qualitative Inquiry," 2021.

242. Kerner, "How Organizations Can Benefit from Friendly Hackers," 2021.

243. Galinkin, "Winning the Ransomware Lottery: A Game-Theoretic Approach to Preventing Ransomware Attacks," 2021.

244. Mohammad, "Ransomware Evolution, Growth and Recommendation for Detection," 2020.

245. Ozer et al., "A Prevention and a Traction System for Ransomware Attacks," 2020.

246. Ozer et al., "A Prevention and a Traction System for Ransomware Attacks," 2020.

247. Akinde et al., "Review of Computer Malware: Detection and Preventive Strategies," 2021.

248. Oz et al., "A Survey on Ransomware: Evolution, Taxonomy, and Defense Solutions," 2022.

249. Alqahtani and Sheldon, "A Survey of Crypto Ransomware Attack Detection Methodologies: An Evolving Outlook," 2022.

250. Kim et al., "Convolutional Neural Network-Based Cryptography Ransomware Detection for Low-End Embedded Processors," 2021.

251. Marks, J. "A Top Cyber Lawmaker is Open to More Regulations for Vital Industries," 2021.

252. The White House, "Fact sheet: Biden-Harris administration delivers on strengthening America's cybersecurity," 2022.

253. The White House, "Fact sheet: Biden-Harris administration delivers on strengthening America's cybersecurity," 2022.

254. Goldsmith, "Red lines for Russia," 2022.

255. Department of the Treasury, "United States and United Kingdom Sanction Members of Russia-Based Trickbot Cybercrime Gang," 2023.

256. Keary, "Rebuffing Russian Ransomware: How the United States Should Use the Colonial Pipeline and JBS USA Hackings as a Defense Guide for Ransomware," 2022.

257. Baram, "US Global Ransomware Summit: More Needs to be Done," 2021.

258. Baram, "US Global Ransomware Summit: More Needs to be Done," 2021.

259. Baram, "US Global Ransomware Summit: More Needs to be Done," 2021.
260. Department of Homeland Security, "Secure Cyberspace and Critical Infrastructure," 2022.
261. Jasper, "Restraining Russian Ransomware," 2022.
262. Comizio et al., "Combating Ransomware: One Year On," 2023.
263. Stavridis, "The US military needs to create a cyber force," 2023.
264. Stavridis, "The US military needs to create a cyber force," 2023.
265. Stavridis, "The US military needs to create a cyber force," 2023.
266. Stavridis, "The US military needs to create a cyber force," 2023.
267. Under Secretary of Defense for Policy, "Assistant Secretary of Defense for Homeland Defense and Global Security | Roles & Responsibilities," 2020.
268. Under Secretary of Defense for Policy, "Assistant Secretary of Defense for Homeland Defense and Global Security | Roles & Responsibilities," 2020.
269. Graham, "U.S. Cyber Force: One War Away," 2016.
270. Graham, "U.S. Cyber Force: One War Away," 2016.
271. Winn, "U.S. Can't Wait Any Longer for a Cyber Force," 2022.
272. Winn, "U.S. Can't Wait Any Longer for a Cyber Force," 2022.
273. Winn, "U.S. Can't Wait Any Longer for a Cyber Force," 2022.
274. Winn, "U.S. Can't Wait Any Longer for a Cyber Force," 2022.
275. Winn, "U.S. Can't Wait Any Longer for a Cyber Force," 2022.
276. Winn, "U.S. Can't Wait Any Longer for a Cyber Force," 2022.
277. Burt, "US Defense Tech Veterans Call for a Separate Cyber Force," 2023.
278. Burt, "US Defense Tech Veterans Call for a Separate Cyber Force," 2023.
279. Burt, "US Defense Tech Veterans Call for a Separate Cyber Force," 2023.
280. Malwarebytes, "Glossary: Big-Game Hunting (BGH)," n.d.
281. CrowdStrike, "What is Cyber Big Game Hunting?" 2023.
282. Gihon, "Ransomware Gangs Focus on 'Big Game' Attacks," 2022.
283. Packetlabs, "What is Big Game Hunting?" 2021.
284. Pereira, "'Big Game Hunting' and Geopolitics are Drivers in a Record Year of Ransomware Extortions," 2023.
285. Shea and Harford, "The History and Evolution of Ransomware," 2021.
286. Coveware, "Big Game Hunting is Back Despite Decreasing Ransom Payment Amounts," 2023.
287. Waldman, "Ransomware Groups Shift from Big Game Hunting," 2022.

288. Shea and Harford, "The History and Evolution of Ransomware," 2021.
289. Baker, "How Ransomware Spread: Top 10 Infection Methods," 2023.
290. Sjouwerman, "Why Ransomware Attacks Are So Successful and What Your Business Can Do to Prevent Them," 2022.
291. Shinkman, "Russia Denies Involvement in Darkside Attack on Colonial Pipeline," 2021.
292. Comparitech, "About Us | Find Out More About Comparitech," 2022.
293. Cloudian, "Cloudian S3-Compatible Object Storage," 2023, August 29.
294. Center for Strategic and International Studies, "About CSIS," n.d.
295. Moody, "Map of Worldwide Ransomware Attacks," 2023.
296. Cloudian, "Ransomware Attack List and Alerts," 2023, October 25.
297. Center for Strategic and International Studies, "Significant Cyber Incidents," 2023.
298. Moody, "Map of Worldwide Ransomware Attacks," 2023.
299. Toulas, "MCNA Dental Data Breach Impacts 8.9 Million People After Ransomware Attack," 2023.
300. Center for Strategic and International Studies, "Significant Cyber Incidents," 2023.
301. James, "Recent Data Breaches List," 2023.
302. Moody, "Map of Worldwide Ransomware Attacks," 2023.
303. Console and Associates, P.C., "Practice Resources, LLC Announces Data Breach Impacting the Information of 924,138 Patients," 2022.
304. Moody, "Map of Worldwide Ransomware Attacks," 2023.
305. Winder, "Cisco Hacked: Ransomware Gang Claims it has 2.8GB of Data," 2022.
306. Moody, "Map of Worldwide Ransomware Attacks," 2023.
307. Griffith, "Russia-Linked Hacker Gang Claims Ransomware Attack on McDonald's," 2022.
308. Moody, "Map of Worldwide Ransomware Attacks," 2023.
309. Auguilar, "Denver Suburb Won't Cough Up Millions in Ransomware Attack that Closed City Hall," 2022.
310. Moody, "Map of Worldwide Ransomware Attacks," 2023.
311. Downs, "Sheriff: Glenn County School District Ransomware Attack Referred to FBI," 2022.

312. Associated Press, "Bernalillo County Reports Suspected Ransomware Attack," 2022.

313. Moody, "Map of Worldwide Ransomware Attacks," 2023.

314. Moody, "Map of Worldwide Ransomware Attacks," 2023.

315. Trobaugh, "Crawford County Reeling From Ransomware Cyberattack," 2022.

316. McKeon, "Lengthy Healthcare Cyberattack Recovery Disrupts MD Department of Health," 2022.

317. Moody, "Map of Worldwide Ransomware Attacks," 2023.

318. Moody, "Map of Worldwide Ransomware Attacks," 2023.

319. The White House, Office of the Press Secretary, "Fact Sheet: Biden-Harris Administration Announces National Cybersecurity Strategy," 2023.

320. Cybersecurity and Infrastructure Security Agency, "CISA Establishes Ransomware Vulnerability Warning Pilot Program," 2023.

321. Department of the Treasury, "Ransomware Trends in Bank Secrecy Act Data Between July 2021 and December 2021: Russia-Related Malware Dominates Ransomware Landscape," 2021.

322. Li and Liao, "Ransomware 2.0," 2020.

323. Marks, G. "That Time Julius Caesar was Kidnapped and Insisted His Captors Increase Their Ransom," 2021.

324. The White House, Office of the Press Secretary, "Fact Sheet: Biden-Harris Administration Announces National Cybersecurity Strategy," 2023.

325. Moody, "Map of Worldwide Ransomware Attacks," 2023.

326. Shinkman, "Russia Denies Involvement in Darkside Attack on Colonial Pipeline," 2021.

327. U.S. Senate Committee on Commerce, Science, and Transportation, "Chair Cantwell on Cyber Threats to Energy Infrastructure: Colonial Pipeline Attack 'The tip of the iceberg'," 2021.

328. Cybersecurity and Infrastructure Security Agency, "CISA Establishes Ransomware Vulnerability Warning Pilot Program," 2023.

Bibliography

Abely, C. (2022). Ransomware, cyber sanctions, and the problem of timing. Boston College Law Review, 63, I.47-I.59. https://ssrn.com/abstract=4106698

Adamov, A., & Carlsson, A. (2017). The state of ransomware. Trends and mitigation techniques. In 2017 IEEE East-West Design & Test Symposium (EWDTS). IEEE.

Afianian, A., Niksefat, S., Sadeghiyan, B., & Baptiste, D. (2019). Malware dynamic analysis evasion techniques: A survey. ACM Computing Surveys, 52(6), 1-28. https://doi.org/10.1145/3365001

Aigner, I., Garai-Fodor, M., & Szemere, T. P. (2022). Singapore's journey as a digit-all-ized and innovative smart nation toward sustainability. 2022 IEEE 10th Jubilee International Conference on Computational Cybernetics and Cyber-Medical Systems (ICCC), 1-6. https://doi.org/10.1109/iccc202255925.2022.9922714

Akinde, O. K., Ilori, A. O., Afolayan, A. O., & Adewuyi, O. B. (2021). Review of computer malware: Detection and preventive strategies. International Journal of Computer Science and Information Security (IJCSIS), 19(11), 49-55. https://doi.org/10.5281/zenodo.5847957

Al Jazeera. (2021, December 6). Global ransomware attacks rise 151%: Canada spy agency. Breaking News, World News and Video from Al Jazeera. https://www.aljazeera.com/news/2021/12/6/hackers-increasingly-target-canada-key-infrastructure-spy-agency

Alenezi, M. N., Alabdulrazzaq, H. K., Alshaher, A. A., & Alkharang, M. M. (2022). Evolution of malware threats and techniques: A review. International Journal of Communication Networks and Information Security (IJCNIS), 12(3), 326-337. https://doi.org/10.17762/ijcnis.v12i3.4723

Alqahtani, A., & Sheldon, F. T. (2022). A survey of crypto ransomware attack detection methodologies: An evolving outlook. Sensors, 22(5), 1837. https://doi.org/10.3390/s22051837

Ambrus, A., Chaney, E., & Salitskiy, I. (2018). Pirates of the Mediterranean: An empirical investigation of bargaining with asymmetric information. Quantitative Economics, 9(1), 217-246. https://doi.org/10.3982/qe655

Anghel, M., & Racautanu, A. (2019). A note on different types of ransomware attacks. International Association for Cryptologic Research. https://www.semanticscholar.org/paper/A-note-on-different-types-of-ransomware-attacks-Anghel-Racautanu/09971c939c639369d11e3de4870e58a3ffd063f9

Anstett, K., Gaydos, N., Krugh, T., M, K., Newton, S., S, M., Ratashak, C., V, K., W, S., Champion, B, D., & Q, S. (2022). Ransomware attacks on critical infrastructure sectors. Department of Homeland Security. https://www.dhs.gov/sites/default/files/2022-09/Ransomware%20Attacks%20.pdf

ARMA International. (n.d.). Most ransomware attacks bypass e-mail filtering. Information Management, January/February 2017, 8. https://imm.arma.org/january-february-2017

Associated Press. (2022, January 5). Bernalillo County reports suspected ransomware attack. U.S. News. https://www.usnews.com/news/best-states/new-mexico/articles/2022-01-05/bernalillo-county-reports-suspected-ransomware-attack

Auguilar, J. (2022, September 22). Denver suburb won't cough up millions in ransomware attack that closed city hall. The Denver Post. https://www.denverpost.com/2022/09/22/wheat-ridge-ransomware-fremont-county-cyber-attack/

Aurangzeb, S., Aleem, M., Iqbal, M. A., & Islam, A. (2017). Ransomware: A survey and trends. Journal of Information Assurance and Security, 12. www.researchgate.net/publication/317380115

Baker, K. (2023, April 5). How ransomware spread: Top 10 infection methods. CrowdStrike. https://www.crowdstrike.com/cybersecurity-101/ransomware/how-ransomware-spreads/

Baldwin, P., Blaney, J., Harbour, G., & Weiss, J. (2022, March 23). Congress passes new cyber incident and ransomware payment reporting legislation. JD Supra. https://www.jdsupra.com/legalnews/congress-passes-new-cyber-incident-and-2486038/

Banisakher, M., Omar, M., & Clare, W. (2019). Critical infrastructure - Perspectives on the role of government in cybersecurity. Journal of Computer Sciences and Applications, 7(1), 37-42. https://doi.org/10.12691/jcsa-7-1-6

Baram, G. (2021). US global ransomware summit: More needs to be done. Rajaratnam School of International Studies, 166. http://hdl.handle.net/11540/14428

Barnes, J. E. (2021, September 10). Russia influences hackers but stops short of directing them, report says (Published 2021). The New York Times - Breaking News, US News, World News and Videos. https://www.nytimes.com/2021/09/09/us/politics/russia-ransomware-hackers.html

The Biden administration cracks down on ransomware. (2022). American Journal of International Law, 116(2), 445-451. https://doi.org/10.1017/ajil.2022.12

Blessing, J. (2020). The diffusion of cyber forces: Military innovation and the dynamic implementation of cyber force structure [Doctoral dissertation]. https://surface.syr.edu/etd/1190/

Boeke, S. (2017). National cyber crisis management: Different European approaches. Governance, 31(3), 1-16. https://doi.org/10.1111/gove.12309

Buchanan, S. S. (2022). Cyber-attacks to industrial control systems since Stuxnet: A systematic review (29163646) [Doctoral dissertation]. ProQuest Dissertations and Theses Global.

Burt, J. (2023, April 6). US defense tech veterans call for a separate cyber force. The Register: Enterprise Technology News and Analysis. https://www.theregister.com/2023/04/06/us_cyber_force/

Burt-Miller, J. J. (2021). Exploring cybersecurity expert recommendations to fortify U.S. national security: A generic qualitative inquiry (28863909) [Doctoral dissertation]. ProQuest Dissertations and Theses Global.

Bushwick, S. (2023, January 31). FBI takes down Hive criminal ransomware group. Scientific American. https://www.scientificamerican.com/article/fbi-takes-down-hive-criminal-ransomware-group1/

Callimachi, R. (2014, July 29). Paying ransoms, Europe bankrolls Qaeda terror. The New York Times - Breaking News, US News, World News and Videos. https://www.nytimes.com/2014/07/30/world/africa/ransoming-citizens-europe-becomes-al-qaedas-patron.html

Cambridge Dictionary. (n.d.). Ransom. https://dictionary.cambridge.org/us/dictionary/english/ransom

Canada.ca. (2018, August 15). Canadian Centre for Cyber Security. https://www.cyber.gc.ca/en/about-cyber-centre

Canada.ca. (2023, February 27). Canadian Centre for Cyber Security. https://www.cyber.gc.ca/en

Carmack, D. (2021). For cybersecurity, the best defense is a good offense (3670). The Heritage Foundation. https://report.heritage.org/bg3670

Center for Strategic and International Studies. (2023, November 10). Significant cyber incidents. https://www.csis.org/programs/strategic-technologies-program/significant-cyber-incidents

Center for Strategic and International Studies. (n.d.). About CSIS. https://www.csis.org/about

Cloudian. (2023, August 29). Cloudian S3-compatible object storage. https://cloudian.com/company/

Cloudian. (2023, October 25). Ransomware attack list and alerts. https://cloudian.com/ransomware-attack-list-and-alerts/

Columbus, L. (2021, November 14). Ransomware attacks are getting more complex and even harder to prevent. VentureBeat. https://venturebeat.com/security/ransomware-attacks-are-getting-more-complex-and-even-harder-to-prevent/

Comizio, V. G., Corn, G., Deckelman, W., Hopkins, K., Hughes, M., McCarty, P., Raman, S., Sanger, K., Schwartz, A., Teplinsky, M., & Colling, J. (2023). Combating ransomware: One year on. American University Washington College of Law. https://digitalcommons.wcl.american.edu/research/83/

Comparitech. (2022, October 17). About us | Find out more about Comparitech. https://www.comparitech.com/about-us/

Console and Associates, P.C. (2022, August 19). Practice resources, LLC announces data breach impacting the information of 924,138 patients. JD Supra. https://www.jdsupra.com/legalnews/practice-resources-llc-announces-data-3249085/

Constitutional Rights Foundation. (n.d.). BRIA 18 1 a The United States and the Barbary Pirates. https://www.crf-usa.org/bill-of-rights-in-action/bria-18-1-a-the-united-states-and-the-barbary-pirates.html

Costello, J., & McReynolds, J. (2018). China's strategic support force: A force for a new era. Institute for National Strategic Studies, National Defense University. https://ndupress.ndu.edu/Media/News/Article/1651760/chinas-strategic-support-force-a-force-for-a-new-era/

Coveware. (2023, April 30). Big game hunting is back despite decreasing ransom payment amounts. https://www.coveware.com/blog/2023/4/28/big-game-hunting-is-back-despite-decreasing-ransom-payment-amounts

Crowdstrike. (2022, October 10). A brief history of ransomware [including attacks]. https://www.crowdstrike.com/cybersecurity-101/ransomware/history-of-ransomware/

CrowdStrike. (2023, June 6). What is cyber big game hunting? - CrowdStrike. https://www.crowdstrike.com/cybersecurity-101/cyber-big-game-hunting/

Custers, B., Oerlemans, J. J., & Pool, R. (2020). Laundering the profits of ransomware: Money laundering methods for vouchers and cryptocurrencies. European Journal of Crime, Criminal Law & Criminal Justice, 28, 121-152. https://doi.org/10.1163/15718174-02802002

Cybersecurity and Infrastructure Security Agency Act of 2018, Pub. L. No. 115-278. (2018). https://www.govinfo.gov/content/pkg/COMPS-15296/pdf/COMPS-15296.pdf

Cybersecurity and Infrastructure Security Agency. (2023, March 13). CISA establishes ransomware vulnerability warning pilot program. https://www.cisa.gov/news-events/news/cisa-establishes-ransomware-vulnerability-warning-pilot-program

Cybersecurity and Infrastructure Security Agency. (n.d.-a). About CISA. https://www.cisa.gov/about

Cybersecurity and Infrastructure Security Agency. (n.d.-b). Energy sector. CISA. https://www.cisa.gov/topics/critical-infrastructure-security-and-resilience/critical-infrastructure-sectors/energy-sector

Defense Information System Agency. (n.d.). About DISA. https://www.disa.mil/About

Department of Defense. (2018). Department of Defense Cyber Strategy 2018. https://media.defense.gov/2018/Sep/18/2002041658/-1/-1/1/CYBER_STRATEGY_SUMMARY_FINAL.PDF

Department of Defense. (2021). DOD Dictionary of Military and Associated Terms. https://www.jcs.mil/Portals/36/Documents/Doctrine/pubs/dictionary.pdf

Department of Homeland Security. (2022, February 23). Secure cyberspace and critical infrastructure. https://www.dhs.gov/secure-cyberspace-and-critical-infrastructure

Department of Homeland Security. (2023, May 30). Cybersecurity. https://www.dhs.gov/topics/cybersecurity

Department of State. (2022, August 30). Cybercrime. https://www.state.gov/cybercrime

Department of the Treasury. (2021, November 1). Ransomware trends in bank secrecy act data between July 2021 and December 2021: Russia-related malware dominates ransomware landscape. https://www.fincen.gov/sites/default/files/2022-11/Financial%20Trend%20Analysis_Ransomware%20FTA%202_508%20FINAL.pdf

Department of the Treasury. (2021, September 21). Treasury takes robust actions to counter ransomware. https://home.treasury.gov/news/press-releases/jy0364

Department of the Treasury. (2023, February 9). United States and United Kingdom sanction members of Russia-based Trickbot cybercrime gang. https://home.treasury.gov/news/press-releases/jy1256

Detotto, C., McCannon, B. C., & Vannini, M. (2014). Understanding ransom kidnappings and their duration. The B.E. Journal of Economic Analysis & Policy, 14(3), 849-871. https://doi.org/10.1515/bejeap-2013-0079

Devanny, J., Dwyer, A., Ertan, A., & Stevens, T. (2021). The national Cybercforce that Britain needs? King's College London. https://www.kcl.ac.uk/policy-institute/research-analysis/national-cyber-force

Downs, B. (2022, May 12). Sheriff: Glenn County school district ransomware attack referred to FBI. Action News Now. https://www.actionnewsnow.com/news/crime/sheriff-glenn-county-school-district-ransomware-attack-referred-to-fbi/article_7fa9d182-d24e-11ec-9b50-8780ed702460.html

Dudley, R. (2019, August 27). The extortion economy: How insurance companies are fueling a rise in ransomware attacks. ProPublica. https://www.propublica.org/article/the-extortion-economy-how-insurance-companies-are-fueling-a-rise-in-ransomware-attacks

Dutton, Y. (2019). Funding terrorism: The problem of ransom payments. San Diego Law Review, 53(2), 335-368. https://doi.org/10.31228/osf.io/u29e3

Encyclopedia Britannica. (2019, January 25). The time Julius Caesar was captured by pirates. https://www.britannica.com/story/the-time-julius-caesar-was-captured-by-pirates

Epps, D. L. (2021). Offensive cyber operations reshaping the modern battlespace (28721114) [Master's thesis]. ProQuest Dissertations and Theses Global.

Federal Bureau of Investigation. (2016, May 3). Terrorism. https://www.fbi.gov/investigate/terrorism

Federal Bureau of Investigation. (2022, April 6). Director Christopher Wray announces actions to disrupt and prosecute Russian criminal activity. https://www.fbi.gov/news/press-releases/director-christopher-wray-announces-actions-to-disrupt-and-prosecute-russian-criminal-activity-040622

Federal Bureau of Investigation. (n.d.). National Cyber Investigative Joint Task Force. https://www.fbi.gov/investigate/cyber/national-cyber-investigative-joint-task-force

Fernando, D. W., Komninos, N., & Chen, T. (2020). A study on the evolution of ransomware detection using machine learning and deep learning techniques. IoT, 1(2), 551-604. https://doi.org/10.3390/iot1020030

Financial Crimes Enforcement Network. (2021). Financial trend analysis: Ransomware trends in Bank Secrecy Act data between January 2021 and June 2021. https://www.fincen.gov/sites/default/files/2021-10/Financial%20Trend%20Analysis_Ransomware%20508%20FINAL.pdf

Ford, E. W. (2021). Cyber ransom in the Information Age: A call to arms against the hackers. Journal of Healthcare Management, 66(4), 243-245. https://doi.org/10.1097/jhm-d-21-00161

Fremont-Barnes, G. (2014). The wars of the Barbary pirates: To the shores of Tripoli: the rise of the US Navy and Marines. Bloomsbury Publishing.

Galinkin, E. (2021). Winning the ransomware lottery: A game-theoretic approach to preventing ransomware attacks. In Decision and Game Theory for Security: 12th International Conference, GameSec 2021, virtual event, October 25–27, 2021, proceedings (p. 195–207). Association for Computing Machinery: ACM Digital Library. https://dl.acm.org/doi/abs/10.1007/978-3-030-90370-1_11

Gihon, S. (2022, June 23). Ransomware gangs focus on 'big game' attacks. CyberRisk Alliance. https://www.scmagazine.com/perspective/ransomware-gangs-focus-on-big-game-attacks

Goldsmith, J. (2022). Red lines for Russia. Hoover Digest, Winter 2022, (1), 129-134. https://www.hoover.org/research/red-lines-russia

Graham, M. (2016). U.S. Cyber Force: One war away. Military Review, May-June 2016, 111-118. https://www.armyupress.army.mil/Journals/Military-Review/English-Edition-Archives/May-June-2016/

Griffith, K. (2022, October 11). Russia-linked hacker gang claims ransomware attack on McDonald's. Mail Online. https://www.dailymail.co.uk/news/article-10553013/Russia-linked-hacker-gang-claims-ransomware-attack-McDonalds.html

Hagen, C. (2013, December 9). The story behind the first ransom note in American history. Smithsonian Magazine. https://www.smithsonianmag.com/history/the-story-behind-the-first-ransom-note-in-american-history-180948612/

Heaven, D. (2018). Can you spot the cryptocrime in this picture? MIT Technology Review, 121(3), 58-63. https://www.thefreelibrary.com/Can+you+spot+the+cybercrime+in+this+picture%3F+A+growing+number+of...-a0538787946

Hernandez-Castro, J., Cartwright, E., & Stepanova, A. (2017). Economic analysis of ransomware. SSRN Electronic Journal. https://doi.org/10.2139/ssrn.2937641

History of Information. (n.d.). Dr. Joseph Popp writes the AIDS Trojan horse, the first known ransomware cyber attack. Jeremy M. Norman. https://www.historyofinformation.com/detail.php?id=5135

Holt, T. J., Strumsky, D. A., & Smirnova, O. (2012). Examining the social networks of malware writers and hackers. International Journal of Cyber Criminology, 6(1), 891-903. https://www.researchgate.net/publication/265260799_Examining_the_Social_Networks_of_Malware_Writers_and_Hackers

Hull, G., John, H., & Arief, B. (2019). Ransomware deployment methods and analysis: Views from a predictive model and human responses. Crime Science, 8(1). https://doi.org/10.1186/s40163-019-0097-9

Hunter, B. (2022). 'til the next zero-day comes. Safety-Critical Systems eJournal, 1(1). https://scsc.uk/journal/index.php/scsj/article/view/5

IBM. (2023, February 22). IBM report: Ransomware persisted despite improved detection in 2022. IBM Newsroom. https://newsroom.ibm.com/2023-02-22-IBM-Report-Ransomware-Persisted-Despite-Improved-Detection-in-2022

Insikt Group. (2021, September 9). Dark covenant: Connections between the Russian | Recorded future state and criminal actors. Recorded Future: Securing Our World With Intelligence. https://www.recordedfuture.com/russian-state-connections-criminal-actors

James, K. (2023, September 18). Recent data breaches list - April 2023. Cybersecurity For Me. https://cybersecurityforme.com/recent-data-breaches-list/

Jasper, S. (2022, August 25). Restraining Russian ransomware. Foreign Policy Research Institute. https://www.fpri.org/article/2022/08/restraining-russian-ransomware/

Jenkins, B. M. (2014, September 2). Why the U.S. swaps prisoners but doesn't pay ransom. Rand Corporation. https://www.rand.org/blog/2014/09/why-the-us-swaps-prisoners-but-doesnt-pay-ransom.html

Jenkins, B. M. (2018). Does the U.S. no-concessions policy deter kidnappings of Americans? Rand Corporation. https://doi.org/10.7249/PE277

Keary, J. (2022). Rebuffing Russian ransomware: How the United States should use the Colonial Pipeline and JBS USA hackings as a defense guide for ransomware. Seton Hall University. https://scholarship.shu.edu/student_scholarship/1274

Keith, T. (2021, June 16). Biden and Putin say their summit was constructive as the world waits for results. NPR. https://www.npr.org/2021/06/16/1005679092/what-you-need-to-know-about-bidens-meeting-with-putin

Kerner, S. M. (2021, February 2). How organizations can benefit from friendly hackers. eWEEK. https://www.eweek.com/security/why-organizations-should-embrace-friendly-hackers/

Kim, H., Park, J., Kwon, H., Jang, K., & Seo, H. (2021). Convolutional neural network-based cryptography ransomware detection for low-end embedded processors. Mathematics, 9(7), 705. https://doi.org/10.3390/math9070705

Kyung-shick, C., Scott, T. M., & LeClair, D. P. (2016). Ransomware against police: Diagnosis of risk factors via application of cyber-routine activities theory. International Journal of Forensic Science & Pathology, 253-258. https://doi.org/10.19070/2332-287x-1600061

Leinhos, L. (2020). Cyber defence in Germany: Challenges and the way forward for the Bundeswehr. Connections: The Quarterly Journal, 19(1), 9-19. https://doi.org/10.11610/connections.19.1.02

Lennox-Gentle, T. (2010). Piracy, sea robbery, and terrorism: Enforcing laws to deter ransom payments and hijacking. Transportation Law Journal, 37(3), 199-217. https://digitalcommons.du.edu/tlj/vol37/iss3/3/

Li, Z., & Liao, Q. (2020). Ransomware 2.0. Proceedings of the 15th International Conference on Availability, Reliability and Security. https://doi.org/10.1145/3407023.3409196

Lyngaas, S. (2022, November 14). Microsoft blames Russian military-linked hackers for ransomware attacks in Poland and Ukraine | CNN politics. CNN. https://edition.cnn.com/2022/11/10/politics/microsoft-russian-linked-hackers-poland-ukraine/index.html

Macaulay, T. (2019). The danger of critical infrastructure interdependency. Centre for International Governance Innovation. https://www.jstor.org/stable/resrep26129.16

Malwarebytes. (n.d.). Glossary: Big-game hunting (BGH). https://www.malwarebytes.com/glossary/big-game-hunting-bgh

Marks, G. (2021, March 3). That time Julius Caesar was kidnapped and insisted his captors increase their ransom. Entrepreneur. https://www.entrepreneur.com/growing-a-business/that-time-julius-caesar-was-kidnapped-and-insisted-his/366089

Marks, J. (2021, October 27). A top cyber lawmaker is open to more regulations for vital industries. The Washington Post. https://www.washingtonpost.com/politics/2021/10/27/top-cyber-lawmaker-is-open-more-regulations-vital-industries/

Mat, S. R., Ab Razak, M. F., Kahar, M. N., Arif, J. M., Mohamad, S., & Firdaus, A. (2021). Towards a systematic description of the field using bibliometric analysis: Malware evolution. Scientometrics, 126(3), 2013-2055. https://doi.org/10.1007/s11192-020-03834-6

Matthews, R., & Timur, F. B. (2023). Singapore's 'Total defence' strategy. Defence and Peace Economics, 1-21. https://doi.org/10.1080/10242694.2023.2187924

McGrath, T. (2015, January 21). These are the countries that have (probably) paid hostage ransom to the Islamic State. The World from PRX. https://theworld.org/stories/2015-01-21/these-are-countries-have-probably-paid-hostage-ransom-islamic-state

McKeon, J. (2022, February 9). Lengthy healthcare cyberattack recovery disrupts MD Department of Health. TechTarget: Health IT Security. https://healthitsecurity.com/news/lengthy-healthcare-cyberattack-recovery-disrupts-md-department-of-health

McLaughlin, J. (2023, January 26). FBI says it 'hacked the hackers' to shut down major ransomware group. NPR. https://www.npr.org/2023/01/26/1151696092/fbi-says-it-hacked-the-hackers-to-shut-down-major-ransomware-group

Merriam-Webster. (n.d.-a). Definition of cybercriminal. Dictionary by Merriam-Webster. https://www.merriam-webster.com/dictionary/cybercriminal

Merriam-Webster. (n.d.-b). Definition of cyberterrorism. Dictionary by Merriam-Webster. https://www.merriam-webster.com/dictionary/cyberterrorism

Merriam-Webster. (n.d.-d). Definition of ransom. https://www.merriam-webster.com/dictionary/ransom

Merriam-Webster. (n.d.-c). Definition of ransomware. https://www.merriam-webster.com/dictionary/ransomware

Meyer, J. (2013, June 19). Why the G8 pact to stop paying terrorist ransoms probably won't work—and isn't even such a great idea. Quartz. https://qz.com/95618/why-the-g8-pact-to-stop-paying-terrorist-ransoms-probably-wont-work-and-isnt-even-such-a-great-idea

Mohammad, A. H. (2020). Ransomware evolution, growth and recommendation for detection. Modern Applied Science, 14(3), 68. https://doi.org/10.5539/mas.v14n3p68

Moody, R. (2023, November 10). Map of worldwide ransomware attacks (updated daily). Comparitech. https://www.comparitech.com/blog/information-security/global-ransomware-attacks/

Moore, R. H. (1987). Posse comitatus revisited: The use of the military in civil law enforcement. Journal of Criminal Justice, 15(5), 375-386. https://doi.org/10.1016/0047-2352(87)90060-2

Muslim, A. K., Dzulkifli, D. Z., Nadhim, M. H., & Abdellah, R. H. (2019). A study of ransomware attacks evolution and prevention. Journal of Social Transformation and Regional Development (JSTARD), 1(1), 18-25. https://publisher.uthm.edu.my/ojs/index.php/jstard/article/view/5503

Nast, C. (2022, November 10). Russia's sway over criminal ransomware gangs is coming into focus. WIRED. https://www.wired.com/story/russia-ransomware-gang-connections/

Nast, C. (2023, February 9). Russia's ransomware gangs are being named and shamed. WIRED. https://www.wired.com/story/conti-trickbot-ransomware-sanctions-uk-us/

National Cyber Security Centre. (n.d.). What we do. https://www.ncsc.gov.uk/section/about-ncsc/what-we-do

National Institute of Standards and Technology. (2023, September 1). Cybersecurity. https://www.nist.gov/cybersecurity

National Institute of Standards and Technology [NIST]. (n.d.). Supervisory control and data acquisition (SCADA) - Glossary. Computer Security Resource Center. https://csrc.nist.gov/glossary/term/supervisory_control_and_data_acquisition

National Security Agency. (n.d.). Cybersecurity. National Security Agency | Central Security Service. https://www.nsa.gov/Cybersecurity/

Nelson, S. D., & Simek, J. W. (2018). Ransomware: How many bitcoins are in your wallet. Law Practice: The Business of Practicing Law, 44(1), 40-43. https://www.mazdigital.com/webreader/53663?page=42

Nershi, K., & Grossman, S. (2022). Assessing the political motivations behind ransomware attacks. In Fourth Annual Research Conference on Empirical Approaches to Anti-Money Laundering and Financial Crime. Central Bank of the Bahamas 2023. https://bahamasamlconference.centralbankbahamas.com/2023

Newman, L. H. (2022, November 10). Russia's sway over criminal ransomware gangs is coming into focus. WIRED. https://www.wired.com/story/russia-ransomware-gang-connections/

Norton LifeLock. (n.d.). When were computer viruses first written, and what were their original purposes? https://us.norton.com/blog/malware/when-were-computer-viruses-first-written-and-what-were-their-original-purposes

Novak, M. (2023, May 4). Ransomware attack on Dallas disrupts 911, court and water systems. Forbes. https://www.forbes.com/sites/mattnovak/2023/05/04/ransomware-attack-on-dallas-disrupts-911-court-and-water-systems/

Nunn, J. (2021, October 14). The Posse Comitatus Act explained. Brennan Center for Justice. https://www.brennancenter.org/our-work/research-reports/posse-comitatus-act-explained

O'Gorman, G., & McDonald, G. (2012). Ransomware: A growing menace. Broadcom. https://www.banadersanlat.com/wp-content/uploads/2012/12/ransomware-a-growing-menace.pdf

O'Sullivan, I. (2022, August 8). Cybercrime in the gaming sector is up 167% year-on-year. Tech.co. https://tech.co/news/cybercrime-in-the-gaming-sector-is-up-167-year-on-year

ODNI Office of Strategic Communications. (n.d.). CTIIC home. Office of the Director of National Intelligence. https://www.dni.gov/index.php/ctiic-home

Oz, H., Aris, A., Levi, A., & Uluagac, A. S. (2022). A survey on ransomware: Evolution, taxonomy, and defense solutions. ACM Computing Surveys, 54(11s), 1-37. https://doi.org/10.1145/3514229

Ozer, M., Varlioglu, S., Gonen, B., & Bastug, M. (2020). A prevention and a traction system for ransomware attacks. In 2019 International Conference on Computational Science and Computational Intelligence (CSCI). Institute of Electrical and Electronics Engineers (IEEE). https://doi.org/10.1109/CSCI49370.2019.00032

Packetlabs. (2021, August 24). What is big game hunting? https://www.packetlabs.net/posts/big-game-hunting/

Pearl, M. (2015, January 27). Where exactly is the rule that says governments can't negotiate with terrorists? VICE. https://www.vice.com/en/article/9bzp5v/where-exactly-is-the-rule-that-says-you-cant-negotiate-with-terrorists-998

Pendino, S., Jahn, R. K., & Pedersen, K. (2022). U.S. cyber deterrence: Bringing offensive capabilities into the light. Campaigning: The Journal of the Joint Forces Staff College, 1-10. https://jfsc.ndu.edu/Media/Campaigning-Journals/Academic-Journals-View/Article/3149856/us-cyber-deterrence-bringing-offensive-capabilities-into-the-light/

Pereira, D. (2023, July 14). "Big game hunting" and geopolitics are drivers in a record year of ransomware extortions. OODA Loop. https://www.oodaloop.com/archive/2023/07/14/big-game-hunting-and-geopolitics-are-drivers-in-a-record-year-of-ransomware-extortions/

Polikarpov, E., Eskov, A., & Anisimov, S. (2019). Trends of malware influence on the integrated IT security systems at critical infrastructure objects. E3S Web of Conferences, 135, 04029. https://doi.org/10.1051/e3sconf/201913504029

Presidential Policy Directive 21. (2013). Critical Infrastructure Security and Resilience. https://obamawhitehouse.archives.gov/the-press-office/2013/02/12/presidential-policy-directive-critical-infrastructure-security-and-resil

Radauskas, G. (2023, February 13). Russia wants to legalize cybercrime for homeland. Cybernews – Latest Cybersecurity and Tech News, Research & Analysis. https://cybernews.com/news/russia-cybercrime-for-homeland/

Richardson, R., & North, M. M. (2017). Ransomware: Evolution, mitigation and prevention. International Management Review, 13(1), 1--21. https://digitalcommons.kennesaw.edu/facpubs/4276/

Richardson, R., North, M. M., & Garofalo, D. (2021). Ransomware: The landscape is shifting-a concise report. International Management Review, 17(1), 5-8. https://www.proquest.com/openview/69a0854375fcfb2eb606fe24b846feca/1?pq-origsite=gscholar&cbl=28202

Ryan, I., Roedig, U., & Stol, K. (2022). Insecure software on a fragmenting internet. 2022 Cyber Research Conference - Ireland (Cyber-RCI). https://doi.org/10.1109/cyber-rci55324.2022.10032675

Sabin, S. (2023, May 8). Colonial Pipeline ransomware attack's unexpected legacy. Axios. https://www.axios.com/2023/05/08/colonial-pipeline-ransomware-attacks-unexpected-legacy

Sahay, S. K., Sharma, A., & Rathore, H. (2019). Evolution of malware and its detection techniques. Information and Communication Technology for Sustainable Development, 139-150. https://doi.org/10.1007/978-981-13-7166-0_14

Sanger, D. E. (2021, October 15). U.S. holds global meeting to fight ransomware, minus the world's No. 1 culprit. The New York Times - Breaking News, US News, World News and Videos. https://www.nytimes.com/2021/10/14/us/politics/global-ransomware-meeting.html

Scroxton, A. (2022, March 16). Biden signs ransomware reporting mandate into law. ComputerWeekly.com. https://www.computerweekly.com/news/252514695/Biden-signs-ransomware-reporting-mandate-into-law

Scroxton, A. (2022, March 3). Boardroom does not see ransomware as a priority. ComputerWeekly.com. https://www.computerweekly.com/news/252514125/Boardroom-does-not-see-ransomware-as-a-priority

Sears, A. A. (2021). Ransomware: A bibliometric research study. SLIS Connecting, 10(2), 73-81. https://doi.org/10.18785/slis.1002.08

Sengupta, K. (2020, January 10). UK is about to launch force to hit hostile countries with cyberattacks. The Independent. https://www.independent.co.uk/news/uk/home-news/cyber-warfare-security-force-iran-crisis-ministry-of-defence-a9278591.html

Serwin, A., Meshulam, D., & Javanshir, L. (2022, March 14). US Senate unanimously passes the Strengthening American Cybersecurity Act. DLA Piper. https://www.dlapiper.com/en/insights/publications/2022/03/us-senate-unanimously-passes-the-strengthening-american-cybersecurity-act

Shea, S., & Harford, I. (2021, October 8). The history and evolution of ransomware. SearchSecurity. https://www.techtarget.com/searchsecurity/feature/The-history-and-evolution-of-ransomware

Shinkman, P. D. (2021, May 11). Russia denies involvement in Darkside attack on Colonial Pipeline. U.S. News & World Report. https://www.usnews.com/news/world-report/articles/2021-05-11/russia-denies-involvement-in-darkside-attack-on-colonial-pipeline

Shortland, A., & Keatinge, T. (2017). Closing the gap: Assessing responses to terrorist-related kidnap-for-ransom. Royal United Services Institute for Defence and Security Studies. https://rusi.org/publication/occasional-papers/closing-gap-assessingresponses-terrorist-related-kidnap-ransom

Shull, A., & Hilt, K. (2021). Securing cyberspace in an age of disruption: A glimpse at the rising threatscape. Canadian International Council, 69(27), 1-13.

Singer, P. W., & Friedman, A. (2014). Cybersecurity: What everyone needs to know. Oxford University Press.

Sjouwerman, S. (2022, July 7). Why ransomware attacks are so successful and what your business can do to prevent them. Fast Company. https://www.fastcompany.com/90764583/why-ransomware-attacks-are-so-successful-and-what-your-business-can-do-to-prevent-them

Stavridis, J. (2023, March 8). The US military needs to create a cyber force. The Washington Post. https://www.washingtonpost.com/business/2023/03/08/the-us-needs-a-seventh-branch-of-the-military-cyber-force/aa72d5dc-bdab-11ed-9350-7c5fccd598ad_story.html

Stent, D. (2018). The great cyber game. New Zealand International Review, 43(5), 6-9. https://search.informit.org/doi/abs/10.3316/informit.869444462419930

Stoddart, K. (2016). UK cyber security and critical national infrastructure protection. International Affairs, 92(5), 1079-1105. https://doi.org/10.1111/1468-2346.12706

Strengthening American Cybersecurity Act of 2022, S.3600, 117th Cong. (2022). https://www.congress.gov/bill/117th-congress/senate-bill/3600/text

Swasey, K. (2020). Insufficient healthcare cybersecurity invites ransomware attacks and sale of PHI on the dark web. Center for Anticipatory Intelligence. https://www.usu.edu/cai/student-research/studentpaper-swasey

Swinhoe, D. (2019, May 30). Why businesses don't report cybercrimes to law enforcement. CSO Online. https://www.csoonline.com/article/3398700/why-businesses-dont-report-cybercrimes-to-law-enforcement.html

Tate, R., & Bates, C. (2022). Deterrence thru transparent offensive cyber persistence. The Cyber Defense Review, 7(4), 227-246. https://www.jstor.org/stable/10.2307

Testament Press. (n.d.). Ancient money calculator. https://testamentpress.com/ancient-money-calculator.html

Thomas, D. S. (2021, November 10). Cybercrime: It's worse than we thought. NIST. https://www.nist.gov/blogs/taking-measure/cybercrime-its-worse-we-thought

Tidy, J. (2021, July 3). US companies hit by 'colossal' cyber-attack. BBC News. https://www.bbc.com/news/world-us-canada-57703836

Tidy, J. (2023, February 9). Seven Russians sanctioned over ransomware cyber-crime. BBC News. https://www.bbc.com/news/technology-64586361

Toulas, B. (2023, May 29). MCNA dental data breach impacts 8.9 million people after ransomware attack. BleepingComputer. https://www.bleepingcomputer.com/news/security/mcna-dental-data-breach-impacts-89-million-people-after-ransomware-attack/

Trobaugh, J. (2022, January 25). Crawford County reeling from ransomware cyberattack. KNWA FOX24. https://www.nwahomepage.com/news/crawford-county-reeling-from-ransomware-cyberattack/

Tupadha, L. S., & Stamp, M. (2021). Machine learning for malware evolution detection (arXiv:2107.01627). arXiv. https://doi.org/10.48550/arXiv.2107.01627

Uberti, D. (2022, June 2). Russia-linked ransomware groups are changing tactics to dodge crackdowns. WSJ. https://www.wsj.com/articles/russia-linked-ransomware-groups-are-changing-tactics-to-dodge-crackdowns-11654178400

Under Secretary of Defense for Policy. (2020, September 16). Assistant Secretary of Defense for Homeland Defense and Global Security | Roles & Responsibilities. Department of Defense. https://policy.defense.gov/OUSDP-Offices/ASD-for-Homeland-Defense-and-Hemispheric-Affairs/Defense-Critical-Infrastructure-Program/Roles/

United Nations Office of Counter-terrorism, & U.N. Security Council Counter-terrorism Committee Executive Directorate. (2018). The protection of critical infrastructure against terrorist attacks: Compendium of good practices. Interpol. https://www.un.org/securitycouncil/ctc/content/protection-critical-infrastructure-against-terrorist-attacks-compendium-good-practices

United Nations Security Council Counter-Terrorism Committee Executive Directorate [CTED], & United Nations Office of Counter-Terrorism [UNOCT]. (2018). The protection of critical infrastructures against terrorist attacks: Compendium of good practices. United Nations. https://www.un.org/securitycouncil/ctc/sites/www.un.org.securitycouncil.ctc/files/files/documents/2021/Jan/compendium_of_good_practices_eng.pdf

United Nations. (n.d.). About us. https://www.un.org/en/about-us

United States Air Force. (n.d.). 75th SFS force protection. Hill Air Force Base. https://www.hill.af.mil/About-Us/Fact-Sheets/Display/Article/397546/75th-sfs-force-protection/

United States Cyber Command [USCYBERCOM] Public Affairs Office. (2022, October 18). Cyber 101 - U.S. Cyber Command mission. U.S. Cyber Command. https://www.cybercom.mil/Media/News/Article/3192016/cyber-101-us-cyber-command-mission/

United States Cyber Command [USCYBERCOM] Public Affairs. (2021, December 29). 2021: A year in review. U.S. Cyber Command. https://www.cybercom.mil/Media/News/Article/2885401/2021-a-year-in-review/

United States joins with Allies, including NATO, to attribute malicious cyber activities to China. (2021). American Journal of International Law, 115(4), 715-721. https://doi.org/10.1017/ajil.2021.54

United States Secret Service. (n.d.). Cyber investigations. https://www.secretservice.gov/investigations/cyber

United States Secret Service [USSS]. (n.d.-a). Preparing for a cyber incident: A guide to e-skimming. https://www.secretservice.gov/sites/default/files/reports/2020-12/Preparing%20for%20a%20Cyber%20Incident%20-%20A%20Guide%20to%20e-Skimming%20v%201.0.pdf

United States Secret Service [USSS]. (n.d.-b). Preparing for a cyber incident: A guide to ransomware. https://www.secretservice.gov/sites/default/files/reports/2021-11/Preparing%20for%20a%20Cyber%20Incident%20-%20A%20Guide%20to%20Ransomware%20v%201.1.pdf

United States Secret Service [USSS]. (n.d.-c). Preparing for a cyber incident: An introductory guide. https://www.secretservice.gov/sites/default/files/reports/2020-12/Preparing%20for%20a%20Cyber%20Incident%20-%20An%20Introductory%20Guide%20v%201.1.pdf

United States Secret Service [USSS]. (n.d.-d). Preparing for a cyber incident: Anatomy of a business email compromise. https://www.secretservice.gov/sites/default/files/reports/2020-12/Preparing%20for%20a%20Cyber%20Incident%20-%20Anatomy%20of%20a%20Business%20Email%20Compromise%20v%201.0.pdf

United States Secret Service [USSS]. (n.d.-e). Preparing for a cyber incident: Contacting law enforcement. https://www.secretservice.gov/sites/default/files/reports/2020-12/Preparing%20for%20a%20Cyber%20Incident%20-%20Contacting%20Law%20Enforcement%20v%201.0.pdf

United States Secret Service [USSS]. (n.d.-f). Preparing for a cyber incident: Reporting cyber incidents to the federal government. https://www.secretservice.gov/sites/default/files/reports/2020-12/Preparing%20for%20a%20Cyber%20Incident%20-%20Reporting%20Cyber%20Incidents%20to%20the%20Federal%20Government%20v%201.0.pdf

United States Secret Service [USSS]. (n.d.-g). Preparing for a cyber incident. https://www.secretservice.gov/investigation/Preparing-for-a-Cyber-Incident

United States Senate Committee on Commerce, Science, and Transportation. (2021, July 27). Chair Cantwell on cyber threats to energy infrastructure: Colonial pipeline attack "The tip of the iceberg". United States Senate. https://www.commerce.senate.gov/2021/7/chair-cantwell-on-cyber-threats-to-energy-infrastructure-colonial-pipeline-attack-the-tip-of-the-iceberg

Vaczi, D., & Szadeczky, T. (2019). A threat for the trains: Ransomware as a new risk. Interdisciplinary Description of Complex Systems, 17(1), 1-6. https://doi.org/10.7906/indecs.17.1.1

Wadkar, M., Di Troia, F., & Stamp, M. (2020). Detecting malware evolution using support vector machines. Expert Systems with Applications, 143, 113022. https://doi.org/10.1016/j.eswa.2019.113022

Waldman, A. (2022, February 9). Ransomware groups shift from big game hunting. TechTarget: Security. https://www.techtarget.com/searchsecurity/news/252513216/Ransomware-groups-shift-from-big-game-hunting

Warrell, H. (2021, October 25). GCHQ to use new cyber force to hunt ransomware gangs. Financial Times. https://www.ft.com/content/2e391872-428d-44bf-8910-23f123c8aaa6

Weber, V. (2022, July 26). Financial incentives may explain the perceived lack of ransomware in Russia's latest assault on Ukraine. Council on Foreign Relations. https://www.cfr.org/blog/financial-incentives-may-explain-perceived-lack-ransomware-russias-latest-assault-ukraine

The White House, Office of the Press Secretary. (2021, October 13). Fact sheet: Ongoing public U.S. efforts to counter ransomware. [Press release]. https://www.whitehouse.gov/briefing-room/statements-releases/2021/10/13/fact-sheet-ongoing-public-u-s-efforts-to-counter-ransomware/

The White House, Office of the Press Secretary. (2023, March 2). Fact Sheet: Biden-Harris administration announces national cybersecurity strategy. [Press release]. https://www.whitehouse.gov/briefing-room/statements-releases/2023/03/02/fact-sheet-biden-harris-administration-announces-national-cybersecurity-strategy/

The White House. (2018). National cyber strategy of the United States of America. https://trumpwhitehouse.archives.gov/wp-content/uploads/2018/09/National-Cyber-Strategy.pdf

The White House. (2022, October 10). Fact sheet: Biden-Harris administration delivers on strengthening America's cybersecurity. https://www.whitehouse.gov/briefing-room/statements-releases/2022/10/11/fact-sheet-biden-harris-administration-delivers-on-strengthening-americas-cybersecurity/

The White House. (2023). National cyber strategy March 2023. https://www.whitehouse.gov/wp-content/uploads/2023/03/National-Cybersecurity-Strategy-2023.pdf

The White House. (2024, March 1). Office of the National Cyber Director. https://www.whitehouse.gov/oncd/

Williams, K. A. (2022). Conti ransomware gang: An analysis of the group's motives and methods (29391647) [Master's thesis]. ProQuest Dissertations and Theses Global.

Winder, D. (2022, August 13). Cisco hacked: Ransomware gang claims it has 2.8GB of data. Forbes. https://www.forbes.com/sites/daveywinder/2022/08/13/cisco-hacked-ransomware-gang-claims-it-has-28gb-of-data/?sh=5fe593744043

Winn, J. (2022, April 22). U.S. can't wait any longer for a cyber force. National Defense Magazine | NDIA's Business & Technology Magazine. https://www.nationaldefensemagazine.org/articles/2022/4/22/us-cant-wait-any-longer-for-a-cyber-force

Zimba, A., & Chishimba, M. (2019). Understanding the evolution of ransomware: Paradigm shifts in attack structures. International Journal of Computer Network and Information Security, 11(1), 26-39. https://doi.org/10.5815/ijcnis.2019.01.03

Index

Acknowledgments

I never anticipated coming this far when I began this journey. However, I have been fortunate to have years surrounded by family, friends, co-workers, and supervisors who continuously pushed me to excel. I have achieved things I could once only dream of because of the support of these fine people.

I want to thank my wife, Angeletha, for all your years of support. Thank you for your advice and counsel. You stood by me through the many long days and nights I remained buried in my research. Without your support, none of this would have been possible. You never doubted I would make it—even for an instant.

Thank you to my family. Thank you to my parents, Theodore and Margaret, and her husband, Ronald, who guided me to become the man I am today. Thank you to my siblings, Cynthia, James, and Monica, as we mutually pushed one another to greater heights. Thank you to my sons, Shane and Samuel, who continuously challenge me to be more than I am.

I am also grateful for the supervisors and commanding officers who mentored me as I grew professionally. If not for the instructions and counsel of Chris Truss, Michael Snyder, Timothy Hayes, Leo Manahl, Dewey Hansford, Raymund Tembreull, Denniss Turriff, Scott Deeds, and Kevin Lombardo, I may not be the professional I am today. I am eternally grateful for their mentorship. I also want to acknowledge the support of my friends Derrell Perry, Daniel Millage, J. Timothy "Smitty" Smith, Krystal Conrad, McKisa Fryer, and Ashiya "Pebbles" Graves.

Additionally, I wish to express my sincerest appreciation to my committee for their guidance and wisdom. I could complete this work only through the knowledgeable counsel and professional dedication of Dr. Herbert Kemp, Dr. Raymond Curts, Dr. Harry Nimon, and Dr. Beth Eisenfeld.

Thank you.

About the Author

Dr. Duane A. Long is a security professional and national security researcher specializing in transnational security threats, critical infrastructure protection, and international defense cooperation. He currently serves as a Foreign Military Sales Security Specialist with the Weapons Superiority Division of the Air Force Life Cycle Management Center at Robins Air Force Base, Georgia, where he oversees multiple security disciplines in support of the AIM-120 Advanced Medium-Range Air-to-Air Missile (AMRAAM) international program.

Dr. Long began his career in the United States Air Force in 1993 as a Security Police trainee. Over a 24-year career in Security Forces, he served in a wide range of operational and leadership positions, including assignments in California, Japan, Wyoming, Kansas, Hawaii, Texas, and Colorado. His duties included protecting nuclear missile facilities, supporting fighter and intelligence operations, leading security forces units, conducting criminal investigations, and managing installation security and antiterrorism programs. He concluded his military service at Cheyenne Mountain Air Force Station, Colorado, where he held multiple senior leadership roles in installation security, plans and programs, and operations.

After retiring from active duty in 2017, Dr. Long pursued higher education full-time. He earned a Bachelor of Science in Counterterrorism Studies from Henley-Putnam University, a Master of Science in Intelligence Management from National American University, and a Doctor of Strategic Security from National American University in 2024. His doctoral research examined ransomware attacks conducted by Russian cybercriminal organizations against critical infrastructure in the United States.

Dr. Long's professional experience in security operations, combined with his academic research in cybersecurity and national security policy, informs his analysis of emerging cyber threats and strategies for defending critical infrastructure in the digital age.